Kubernetes Design Patterns and Extensions

Enhance your container-cluster management skills and efficiently develop and deploy applications

Onur Yilmaz

BIRMINGHAM - MUMBAI

Kubernetes Design Patterns and Extensions

Acquisitions Editor: Aditya Date
Content Development Editor: Tanmayee Patil
Production Coordinators: Shantanu Zagade, Ratan Pote

First published: September 2018

Production reference: 1260918

Published by Packt Publishing Ltd.
Livery Place
35 Livery Street
Birmingham
B3 2PB, UK.

ISBN 978-1-78961-927-0

www.packtpub.com

Contributor

About the Author

Onur Yilmaz is a software engineer in a multinational enterprise software company. He is a Certified Kubernetes Administrator (CKA) and works on Kubernetes and cloud management systems. He has been developing software systems since he was eleven years old. He is a keen supporter of cutting-edge technologies, such as Docker, Kubernetes, and cloud-native applications. He has one master's and two bachelor's degrees in engineering and is pursuing a doctorate degree.

Packt Is Searching for Authors like You

If you're interested in becoming an author for Packt, please visit authors.packtpub.com and apply today. We have worked with thousands of developers and tech professionals, just like you, to help them share their insight with the global tech community. You can make a general application, apply for a specific hot topic that we are recruiting an author for, or submit your own idea.

`mapt.io`

Mapt is an online digital library that gives you full access to over 5,000 books and videos, as well as industry leading tools to help you plan your personal development and advance your career. For more information, please visit our website.

Why Subscribe?

- Spend less time learning and more time coding with practical eBooks and Videos from over 4,000 industry professionals
- Improve your learning with Skill Plans built especially for you
- Get a free eBook or video every month
- Mapt is fully searchable
- Copy and paste, print, and bookmark content

PacktPub.com

Did you know that Packt offers eBook versions of every book published, with PDF and ePub files available? You can upgrade to the eBook version at `www.Packt.com` and as a print book customer, you are entitled to a discount on the eBook copy. Get in touch with us at `service@packt.com` for more details.

At `www.Packt.com`, you can also read a collection of free technical articles, sign up for a range of free newsletters, and receive exclusive discounts and offers on Packt books and eBooks.

Table of Contents

Preface

Before plunging into how Kubernetes works, this book introduces you to the world of container orchestration and describes the recent changes in application development. It helps you understand the problems that Kubernetes solves and shows how to use Kubernetes resources to deploy applications. You also learn to apply the security model of Kubernetes clusters. The book also describes how services running in Kubernetes can leverage the platform's security features. You learn to troubleshoot Kubernetes clusters and debug Kubernetes applications. You also learn to analyze the networking model and its alternatives in Kubernetes, and apply best practices in Kubernetes with design patterns. By the time you are done reading the book, you will know all about using the power of Kubernetes for managing your containers.

After completing this book, you will be able to:

- Understand and classify software designs patterns per the cloud-native paradigm
- Apply best practices in Kubernetes with design patterns
- Access Kubernetes API programmatically using client libraries
- Extend Kubernetes with custom resources and controllers
- Integrate into access control mechanisms and interact resource lifecycle in Kubernetes
- Develop and run custom schedulers in Kubernetes

Who This Book Is For

If you are interested in configuring and troubleshooting Kubernetes clusters and developing microservices-based applications on Kubernetes clusters, then this is a very useful book for you. DevOps engineers with basic knowledge of Docker will find this book useful.

What This Book Covers

Chapter 1, *Kubernetes Design Patterns*, will help you to understand Kubernetes patterns which would be presented with the examples from Kubernetes itself and external applications.

Chapter 2, *Kubernetes Client Libraries*, will help you to cover accessing Kubernetes API with raw HTTP queries to complex libraries with both in-cluster and out-cluster examples.

Chapter 3, *Kubernetes Extensions*, will present extension capabilities of Kubernetes with custom resource definitions, custom controllers, dynamic admission controllers, and custom schedulers.

To Get the Most out of This Book

We assume that you are comfortable with command-line tools and computer programming concepts and languages. The minimum hardware requirements are: Intel Core i7 or equivalent, 8 GB RAM, 35 GB hard disk, and a stable internet connection. You'll also need the following software installed in advance:

- Access to a Kubernetes cluster with the version equal to or higher than 1.10 Local Kubernetes solutions such as minikube or clusters living in cloud providers: https://github.com/kubernetes/minikube
- Kubernetes command line tool kubectl is required for accessing Kubernetes from terminal:
  https://kubernetes.io/docs/tasks/tools/install-kubectl/
- Docker client and server with the minimum version of 18.03 are required for building and testing the client libraries:
  https://www.docker.com/get-started
- Installing Python and Go are not required, however recommended for playing around with the client libraries locally:
  - https://www.python.org/downloads/
  - https://golang.org/

Download the Example Code Files

You can download the example code files for this book from your account at www.packt.com. If you purchased this book elsewhere, you can visit www.packt.com/support and register to have the files emailed directly to you.

You can download the code files by following these steps:

1. Log in or register at www.packt.com.
2. Select the **SUPPORT** tab.
3. Click on **Code Downloads & Errata**.
4. Enter the name of the book in the **Search** box and follow the onscreen instructions.

Once the file is downloaded, please make sure that you unzip or extract the folder using the latest version of:

- WinRAR/7-Zip for Windows
- Zipeg/iZip/UnRarX for Mac
- 7-Zip/PeaZip for Linux

The code bundle for the book is also hosted on GitHub at https://github.com/TrainingByPackt/Kubernetes-Design-Patterns-and-Extensions. In case there's an update to the code, it will be updated on the existing GitHub repository.

We also have other code bundles from our rich catalog of books and videos available at https://github.com/PacktPublishing/. Check them out!

Conventions Used

There are a number of text conventions used throughout this book.

CodeInText: Indicates code words in text, database table names, folder names, filenames, file extensions, pathnames, dummy URLs, user input, and Twitter handles. Here is an example: "With this method, kubectl securely connects to the API server with its own credentials and creates a proxy for the applications on the local system."

A block of code is set as follows:

```
{
  "apiVersion":"v1",
  "kind":"Namespace",
  "metadata":{
    "name":"packt-client"
  }
}
```

When we wish to draw your attention to a particular part of a code block, the relevant lines or items are set in bold:

```
curl -X POST http://localhost:8080/api/v1/namespaces/  \
--header "Content-Type:application/json" \
```

Activity: These are scenario-based activities that will let you practically apply what you've learned over the course of a complete section. They are typically in the context of a real-world problem or situation.

 Warnings or important notes appear like this.

Get in Touch

Feedback from our readers is always welcome.

General feedback: Email feedback@packtpub.com and mention the book title in the subject of your message. If you have questions about any aspect of this book, please email us at questions@packtpub.com.

Errata: Although we have taken every care to ensure the accuracy of our content, mistakes do happen. If you have found a mistake in this book, we would be grateful if you would report this to us. Please visit www.packt.com/submit-errata, selecting your book, clicking on the Errata Submission Form link, and entering the details.

Piracy: If you come across any illegal copies of our works in any form on the Internet, we would be grateful if you would provide us with the location address or website name. Please contact us at copyright@packt.com with a link to the material.

If you are interested in becoming an author: If there is a topic that you have expertise in and you are interested in either writing or contributing to a book, please visit authors.packtpub.com.

Reviews

Please leave a review. Once you have read and used this book, why not leave a review on the site that you purchased it from? Potential readers can then see and use your unbiased opinion to make purchase decisions, we at Packt can understand what you think about our products, and our authors can see your feedback on their book. Thank you!

For more information about Packt, please visit packt.com.

 All the solutions to the activities are present in the *Appendix* section.

Kubernetes Design Patterns

Design patterns are the formalization of best practices for everyday problems. Using design patterns in everyday, professional life creates a common language and communication platform for you to work on. In real life, seasoned engineers do not explain how to convert one interface into another; instead, they decide to implement an adapter. Design patterns hide the complexity and details of communication and create a common platform. In addition, converting business requirements into code is more comfortable with the accumulated knowledge of design patterns.

Kubernetes is the uprising and prominent open source container orchestration system, designed by Google. Its fundamental features include automation, scaling, and scheduling of containerized applications. To have a scalable and reliable cloud-native application, Kubernetes is a crucial part of your toolset. All levels of companies, from start-ups to large enterprises, are using Kubernetes to install and manage cloud-native applications.

This paradigm shift in software development began by creating microservices instead of chunks of large software systems. The "new" best practices have aligned with the de facto cloud-native orchestration tool, Kubernetes. Throughout this book, Kubernetes design patterns and extension capabilities will be presented. The book starts by explaining best practices to show how to create Kubernetes-native applications. Following that, accessing Kubernetes itself programmatically and enriching the best orchestration tool ever created will be explained. Finally, Kubernetes itself will be extended with a higher level of automation. At the end of the day, you will have the technical knowledge and hands-on experience to not only create applications to run on Kubernetes, but also extend the system itself.

In this first chapter, Kubernetes design patterns will be presented, starting with the fundamentals of design patterns. Following that, you will build Kubernetes solutions using structural patterns, assemble systems with behavioral patterns, and finally, install applications according to the deployment strategies.

By the end of this chapter, you will be able to:

- Define the fundamentals of design patterns
- Explain the classification of patterns
- Use Kubernetes design patterns to solve real-life problems
- Build solutions using structural patterns
- Assemble complex systems with behavioral patterns
- Install applications with deployment strategies

Software Design Patterns

In software development, a design pattern is a repeatable solution to a widespread problem, since it is ubiquitous to solve the same problems you have encountered before. There are two main advantages of design patterns. The first advantage is that they are proven solutions, and the second one is that they create a communication platform between developers. With these advantages, templates and specifications have been formalized over the years to create a knowledge and experience pool.

 Design patterns are not finished designs that can be transformed directly into code – they are only best practices and set of approaches.

Software development is seen as a relatively young and evolving field of study; however, most of the problems solved in various circumstances are similar. For instance, it is common to create a single instance component in various software systems, such as payment systems, log managers, **enterprise resource planning** (ERP) systems, or online games. Therefore, making use of past collected knowledge helps development teams to advance rapidly.

Design patterns and corresponding business requirements could seem artificial and only software-related. However, both problems and solutions have roots in real life. For instance, the singleton pattern is proposed as a best practice for implementing a configuration manager. With the same approach in mind, the adapter pattern is proposed as a best practice to work with both versions of the APIs. As its name implies, it is a similar approach in real-life to using electrical adapters to work with the different plug and socket types in various countries. As these examples indicate, software design patterns and the ideas behind them all come from real-life experiences.

Uses of Software Design Patterns

There are two main uses of design patterns. First, design patterns create a common platform for developers with their terminology. For example, during a technical discussion, let's assume that a design decision is made to use a single instance of a component. All other developers, at least the ones that are aware of design patterns, will not need any further information considering the properties of the singleton pattern. Although this looks trivial, it is an enrichment of communication, with the best practices of technical expertise. Secondly, knowing and leveraging best practices in engineering makes it easier to advance rapidly. Let's imagine that you are designing a car – you should always start by inventing the best wheel possible first. This makes the process faster and eliminates the gains of learning from past
mistakes.

Classification of Software Design Patterns

Design patterns are classified in three ways. With new technologies and programming languages always emerging, new groups are proposed, but the main idea of classification remains the same – the interaction between their controllers
and other applications:

Category	Focus area	Examples
Creational patterns	Instantiation	**Factory method**: Defines a generic interface for object creation and defers customization. **Object pool**: Creates a pool of reusable objects and distributes/collects objects from the pool.
Structural patterns	Composition	**Facade**: Encapsulates interfaces of a complex system into one interface. **Proxy**: Uses placeholder objects that represent other objects.
Behavioral patterns	Communication	**Iterator**: Provides a way of reaching elements of a complex object. **Observer**: Notifies other interested objects when the state of an object changes.

To sum this section up, design patterns are formalized best practices that have roots in both real-life and software design. They create a common communication platform for developers, and they are a valuable source of knowledge as a collection.

In the following chapter, design patterns for Kubernetes are presented as best practices for creating, managing, and deploying modern cloud-native applications.

Kubernetes Design Patterns

The evolution of microservices and container technologies has changed the way software applications are designed, developed, and deployed. Nowadays, modern cloud-native applications focus on scalability, flexibility, and reliability in order to meet business requirements. For instance, the scalability of an application with thousands of instances running in a reliable manner was not a concern 10 years ago. Similarly, self-awareness and self-healing features were out of scope when there was no orchestrator for these issues, such as Kubernetes.

New requirements and cloud-native characteristics unveil their own best practices and design patterns. Extensive use and the adoption of Kubernetes by all sorts of companies, including start-ups and large enterprises, made it possible to formalize and collect best practices. In this section, widely known and essential design patterns and deployment strategies in Kubernetes will be described. With the help of these patterns, you'll be able to make use of the best practices that have been formalized by Kubernetes itself.

Structural Patterns

Structural patterns are focused on the composition of building blocks to create higher-level complex resources. In microservice architecture, applications are packaged and deployed as containers. This approach makes it easier to scale applications with less overhead and more isolation. However, this makes it difficult to schedule and run related containers side-by-side, or sequentially in a cluster with thousands of nodes. For instance, if you want to run your frontend and backend containers together in a cluster, you need to find a mechanism so that you can always schedule them to the same nodes. Likewise, if you need to fill in configuration file templates before starting your application, there is a need to ensure that configuration handler containers are running before the application is.

In Kubernetes, containers are the building blocks that are encapsulated in pods. As a container orchestrator, Kubernetes provides built-in functionalities for organizing containers within pods. In this section, the sidecar and initialization structural design patterns for Kubernetes will be explained.

Pods are the smallest deployable resources in Kubernetes, and they consist of one or more containers sharing resources. Pod containers are always scheduled to the same node so that they can share resources such as networking and storage.
Further information about the pod concept is available in the official documentation of Kubernetes: `https://kubernetes.io/docs/concepts/workloads/pods/pod`.

Sidecar Pattern

Modern software applications often require external functionalities such as monitoring, logging, configuration, and networking. When these functionalities are tightly integrated into the application, they can run as a single process. However, this violates the isolation principle and creates an opportunity for a single point of failure. With this idea, containers in cloud-native applications are expected to follow the Unix philosophy:

- Containers should have one task
- Containers should work together
- Containers should handle text streams

The **single point of failure (SPOF)** is a component within a system where its failure can cause all systems to fail. To have reliable and scalable cloud-native applications, SPOFs are undesirable, and system designs should be checked for their existence.

The Unix philosophy focuses on designing a small operating system with a clean service interface. To have such a system, simple, precise, clear, and modular software development should be undertaken, taking into consideration the developers and maintainers. Besides, the philosophy emphasizes that you should compose subsystems instead of creating a big, monolithic design.

With this idea, it is a conventional approach to separate the main application and run a couple of sidecars attached, which are provided for extra functionality. The main advantages of using a sidecar are as follows:

- They have independent programming languages and runtime dependencies
- They monitor the main application closely and minimize latency
- They extend black box applications

In the following activity, a web-based game will be installed in Kubernetes. As expected, there should be at least one container running the web server. However, there is an additional requirement of continuous source code synchronization.
With the Unix philosophy, it is expected to make containers with only one primary task. They should also work independently and together to achieve the necessary requirements. Finally, these containers should update their statuses, informing the console as log lines. All three of these points are covered in the following activity.

Activity: Running a Web Server with Synchronization

Scenario

You are assigned the task of making a Kubernetes installation for a web-based 2048 game. However, the game is still in development and developers push frequent changes throughout the day. In this installation, the game should be frequently updated to include the recent changes.

Aim

With the successful deployment, there should be a pod running in Kubernetes with two containers. One of the containers should serve the game and the other container, namely the sidecar container, should continuously update the source code of the game. Using Kubernetes, you need to create a cloud-native solution where the server and synchronization tasks are working together, but not depending on each other.

Prerequisites

Use a git Docker image for continuous synchronization in the sidecar container and an open source code repository for the 2048 game.

Steps for Completion

1. Create a pod definition.
2. Include two containers:
   - httpd for game serving.
   - git for source code synchronization.

3. Deploy the pod.
4. Show the logs of the synchronization.
5. Check whether the game has started.

All of the code files for the activities in this chapter are provided on GitHub in the Lesson-1 folder at https://goo.gl/gM8W3p.

You are expected to create a 2048 game, like the one shown in the following screenshot:

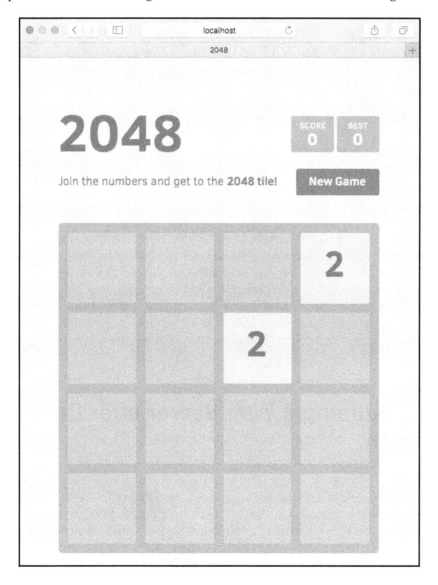

Initialization Pattern

Initialization is a widespread pattern in every part of software engineering, including programming languages and operating systems. In order to handle the initialization of an application in Kubernetes, initialization containers are proposed. Initialization containers, namely **initContainers**, are part of a pod's definition. Separation of concerns is handled by separating the life cycles of containers:

- Init containers
- Main containers

Containers that are defined as initContainers are executed for completion one by one, and they are all expected to exit successfully. After successful completion, the main containers are started. Some of the example uses of startup containers are as follows:

- To create configuration files
- To wait and ensure dependency services are available
- To create volumes and prepare files
- To register services to discovery systems

In the following activity, a web server will be installed in Kubernetes. As expected, there should be at least one container running the web server. However, there is an additional requirement of changing the served files before the web server starts. The life cycle of these operations is separated into the initialization container and the main container. These containers could have different container images and executables; however, they are expected to work on a shared resource. Life cycle separation and working together issues are handled in the following activity, and the initialization pattern is implemented in Kubernetes.

Activity: Running a Web Server after Content Preparation

Scenario

You are assigned the task of making a Kubernetes installation for a web server. However, there are some manual tasks to be carried out to change the files before serving them. You need to ensure that changes are always applied before the content is served. Besides this, show the status of the initialization and check the final output of the web server.

Aim

With the successful deployment, there should be a pod running in Kubernetes with one main container and one initialization container. In the initialization container, write `Welcome from Packt` to the main index file. This file should be served by the main container when started.

Prerequisites

- Use a basic Docker image for the initialization container, such as busybox.
- For the main container, a web server capable image should be used, such as nginx.

Steps for Completion

1. Create a pod definition.
2. Include one initialization container:
   - Change the content of the files.
3. Include one main container:
   - Create a web server.
4. Deploy the pod.
5. Check the status of the initialization container.
6. Check the output of the web server.

You should see the following output:

```
$ curl localhost:8000
Welcome from Packt
$ 
```

All of the code files for the activities in this chapter are provided on GitHub in the `Lesson-1` folder at `https://goo.gl/gM8W3p`.

Behavioral Patterns

In software development, behavioral design patterns focus on the communication and interaction between objects. Interaction and communication includes responsibility assignment, the encapsulation of behaviors, and the delegation of requests. With the microservice architecture, behavioral patterns focus on the communication between microservices and the interaction of services with orchestration tools.

For instance, let's consider the execution of a microservice that checks a user's quota daily. It can be implemented by an infinite loop that includes 24 hours of sleep and the execution of the quota check. Although it works, it consumes additional resources during sleep and creates an inefficient architecture. With the behavioral pattern of the "scheduled job pattern," orchestration tools could handle the scheduling of the microservice and ensure that it runs every 24 hours.

In Kubernetes, containers are encapsulated inside pods, which are the primary interest of behavioral patterns. Behavioral patterns are focused on the interaction and communication of the Kubernetes resources, namely pods, with the Kubernetes services. Communication and interaction within the controller system could include the distribution of pods to nodes, the scheduling of pods, or metadata distribution by the Kubernetes master and node components.

The following behavioral patterns are covered in the following sections:

- The job pattern
- The scheduled job pattern
- The daemon service pattern
- The singleton service pattern
- The introspective pattern

Job Pattern

The general use case of pods in Kubernetes is that they are used for long-running processes that are always up. To this aim, Kubernetes provides higher-level resources such as replication sets or deployments. These high-level resources manage the life cycles of pods by creating replicas, checking for health statuses, and controlling update mechanisms. On the other hand, there is a need for microservices that do one job and successfully exit upon completion. For instance, database initializations, backups, or converting a video should run once and exit without consuming any extra resources. For this requirement, Kubernetes provides a higher-level resource named Job. Kubernetes jobs represent an isolated work run until completion and are ideal for use cases that are required to only run once.

The most important difference between jobs and replication-controlled pods is the `restartPolicy` field:

- For always running pods, the `restartPolicy` is set to `Always`
- For jobs, the `restartPolicy` could be set as `OnFailure` or `Never`

Scheduled Job Pattern

Distributed systems and the microservices architecture do not rely on temporal events for running services; instead, they focus on triggers such as HTTP requests, new database entries, or messaging queues. However, scheduling a task and expecting it to run at specified intervals are common approaches that are part of the "Scheduled Job Pattern". Microservices for maintenance operations, sending daily emails, or checking for old files should be scheduled at fixed intervals and must run to meet business needs. Kubernetes provides the CronJob resource for creating scheduled tasks, and it ensures that these jobs are running.

Daemon Service Pattern

Daemon applications are commonly used in operating systems and programming languages as long-running applications or threads that run as background processes. The names of the daemon applications are httpd, sshd, and containerd; the trailing letter indicates that the services are daemons. Within the microservice architecture, some services should run and scale without any relation to consumer usage. These applications should run on every node in the cluster to ensure the daemon application's requirements, such as:

- **Cluster storage daemons**: glusterd, ceph.
- **Log collection daemons**: fluentd, logstash.
- **Node monitoring daemons**: collectd, Datadog agent, New Relic agent.

In Kubernetes, **DaemonSets** are designed for deploying ongoing background tasks that need to run on all or certain nodes. Without any further management considerations, Kubernetes handles running these daemon pods on the newly joined nodes in the cluster.

Singleton Service Pattern

Running one – and only one – instance is a requirement for applications, since multiple instances could create instability. Although it seems to be against the scalable microservice architecture, there are some applications that are required to follow the singleton pattern:

- Database instances and connectors
- Configuration managers
- Applications that do not scale yet

Kubernetes StatefulSet with a replica count of 1 ensures that only instances of the pod are running in the cluster. With this small configuration, singleton services can be created and used in a cloud-native environment. However, having only one instance of an application in the cluster comes with its drawbacks. For instance, handling the downtime of singleton applications should be handled with care. The primary concern for this issue is how to handle downtime due to the automatic
update of Statefulset. There are two possible solutions in Kubernetes:

- Tolerate occasional downtime during updates
- Set `PodDistruptionBudget` with `minAvailable=1`:
  - Eliminate the automatic update since `PodDistruptionBudget` is set
  - Prepare for disruption by operational steps
  - Delete the `PodDistruptionBudget` resource and let the update continue
  - Recreate `PodDistruptionBudget` for the next disruption

Introspective Pattern

Applications that run on bare-metal clusters know precisely where they are running, the specification of the system, and their network information. This information helps them to work in a self-aware environment. For instance, these applications can align their resource usage, enhance their logs with more data, or send their node-related metric data. In the microservice architecture, applications are considered ephemeral with less dependency than the environment they are running on. However, self-awareness about runtime information, namely the introspective pattern, could increase the utility and discoverability of applications in distributed systems.

In Kubernetes, the Downward API ensures that the following environment and runtime data is provided for the pods:

- **Environment:** Node name, namespace, CPU, and memory limitations.
- **Networking:** Pod IP.
- **Authorization:** Service account.

In the following activity, a simple but self-aware Kubernetes application will be created and installed. The application has all of the runtime information, which is provided by Kubernetes as environment variables. Being a single application, it logs all of these variables to the console. However, the pod definition that's developed throughout this activity shows you how to use the Downward API inside containers to implement an introspective pattern in Kubernetes.

Activity: Injecting Data into Applications

Scenario

You are assigned the task of making a Kubernetes installation for a simple application with self-awareness. In this installation, the application should collect all the runtime information from Kubernetes and write to its logs.

Aim

With the successful deployment, there should be a pod running in Kubernetes with only one container. In this container, all available runtime information should be injected as environment variables. Also, the application should log runtime information.

Prerequisites

Use the Kubernetes Downward API to collect runtime information.

Steps for Completion

1. Create a pod definition with one container:
   - Define the environment variables from the Downward API.
   - Create a shell script to write the environment variables.

2. Deploy the pod.
3. Check the status of the pod.
4. Check the logs of the container.

 All of the code files for the activities in this chapter are provided on GitHub in the `Lesson-1` folder at `https://goo.gl/gM8W3p`.

Deployment Strategies

Designing and developing cloud-native applications with the microservice architecture is essential for reliable and scalable applications of the future. Likewise, deploying and updating applications in the cloud is as critical as design and development. There are various techniques for delivering applications, and therefore choosing the right setup is essential to leverage the impact of change on the consumers. Using the right subset of Kubernetes resources and choosing an appropriate deployment strategy, scalable and reliable cloud-native applications are feasible.

In this section, the following deployment strategies are presented, and you are expected to complete these exercises so that they can see the Kubernetes resources in action:

- Recreate strategy
- Rolling update strategy
- Blue/green strategy
- A/B testing strategy

Recreate Strategy

The recreate strategy is based on the idea of closing old version instances and then creating the next version's. With this strategy, it is inevitable to have downtime, depending on both the shutdown and start duration of applications. In Kubernetes, the recreate strategy can be used for creating deployment resources with the strategy of recreate.

The rest of the operations are handled by Kubernetes. Under the hood, the steps of the recreate strategy are as follows:

1. Requests from users are routed to **V1** instances by using a load balancer:

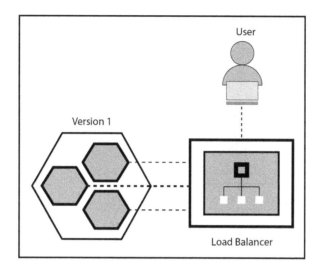

2. **V1** instances are closed, and downtime has started since there is no available instance:

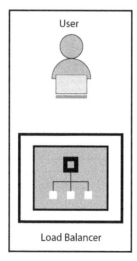

3. **V2** instances are created; however, they are not serving to the requests until they are ready:

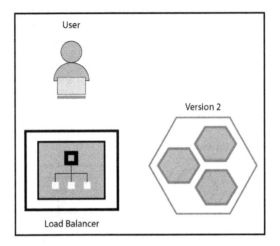

4. Requests from users are routed to **V2** instances:

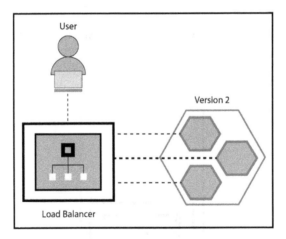

The primary benefits of the recreate strategy are that it's straightforward and not doesn't have any overhead processes. Besides this, the instances are completely renewed with every update, and there is not a time where two versions are running together. However, the downside of this strategy is an inevitable downtime during the update.

Deploying the Application Using the Recreate Strategy

You are running a high-available application on Kubernetes that needs a deployment strategy to handle updates. This application can resist the short span of downtimes; however, there should not be any moment where two versions are running together. This application consumes services that cannot handle working with two different versions at the same time. We want to run an application with the recreate deployment strategy so that updates will be handled by Kubernetes by deleting old instances and creating new ones.

 You can find the `recreate.yaml` file at: https://goo.gl/2woHbx.

Let's begin by following these steps:

1. Create the deployment with the following command:

```
kubectl apply -f recreate.yaml
```

2. In a separate terminal, watch for the deployment changes and wait until all three are available:

```
kubectl get deployment recreate -w
```

3. Update the version of the deployment:

```
kubectl patch deployment recreate -p
'{"spec":{"template":{"spec":{"containers":[{"name":"nginx",
"image":"nginx:1.11"}]}}}}'
```

4. In the terminal that we opened in *Step 2*, it is expected that you should see the deletion of the pods and the downtime, where `Available` reaches zero. Afterward, the creation of new instances can be tracked, where `Available` increases from 0 to 3:

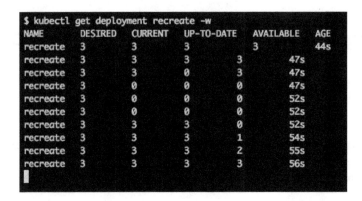

5. You can run the following command for cleanup:

```
kubectl delete -f recreate.yaml
```

Rolling Update Strategy

The rolling update strategy, which is also known as incremental or ramped, is based on the idea of slowly rolling out a version by replacing the previous ones. In this strategy, firstly, a pool of applications is running behind a load balancer. Then, new version instances are started, and when they are up and running, the load balancer redirects requests to the new instances. At the same time, instances from the previous versions are shut down. In Kubernetes, the rolling update strategy is the default strategy in deployments, so any update on the *deployment* is already implementing the rolling update strategy.

While Kubernetes handles this, the steps of the rolling strategy can be tracked as follows:

1. Requests from users are routed to **V1** instances by using a load balancer:

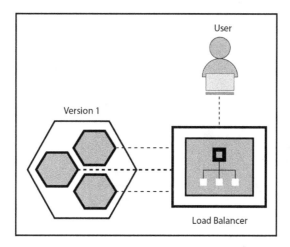

2. **V2** instances are created, and users are directed to them. At the same time, **V1** instances are deleted. During this stage, both versions are running and serving requests:

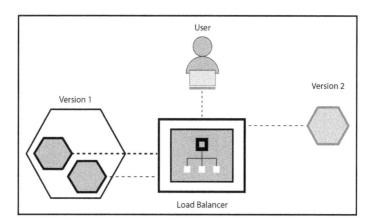

3. Creating **V2** instances and the deletion of **V1** instances is done one at a time until there are no **V1** instances left:

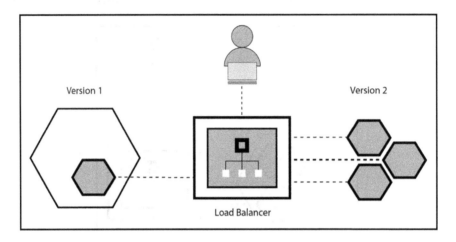

4. Finally, all requests from all users are routed to **V2** instances:

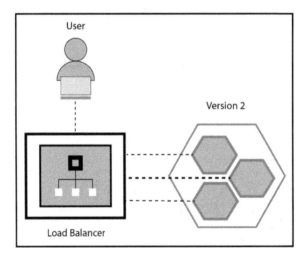

The main advantage of the rolling update strategy is that it is easy and is the default approach of Kubernetes. It is also beneficial for a slow release of new versions by balancing the load during the startup of new instances. On the other hand, Kubernetes automatically handles rollout and rollback, and the duration of these operations are not known. One of the most complicated problems in rolling updates is that two versions are running at the same time in the cluster, and the traffic is not under control.

Deploying an Application Using the Rolling Update Strategy

You are running a high-available application on Kubernetes that needs a deployment strategy to handle updates. This application, let's say, the frontend of your client's company, should always be available so that downtime is out of the question. Multiple versions of the applications could be working together at any time; however, the client does not want to cover the cost of extra resources during the update. We'll run an application with the rolling update deployment strategy so that updates will be handled by Kubernetes by incrementally creating new instances and deleting old instances, one after another. Let's begin by following these steps:

1. Create the deployment with the following command:

   ```
   kubectl apply -f rolling.yaml
   ```

2. In a separate terminal, start a cURL instance in the Kubernetes cluster:

   ```
   kubectl run curl --image=tutum/curl --rm -it
   ```

3. When the Command Prompt is ready, watch for the version of the deployment by using an HTTP request:

   ```
   while sleep 0.5; do curl -s http://rolling/version | grep nginx;
   done
   ```

4. Update the version of the deployment with the following command:

   ```
   kubectl patch deployment rolling -p
   '{"spec":{"template":{"spec":{"containers":[{"name":"nginx",
   "image":"nginx:1.11"}]}}}}'
   ```

5. In the terminal that we opened in *Step 2*, it is expected that we should see Kubernetes handle an incremental change of versions. During the update, there is no interruption of the service. However, both versions are alive and serving requests as 1.10.3 and 1.11.13, and are used interchangeably:

```
root@curl-54988bf969-v62vz:/# while sleep 0.5; do curl -s http://blue-green/version | grep nginx; done
<hr><center>nginx/1.10.3</center>
<hr><center>nginx/1.10.3</center>
<hr><center>nginx/1.10.3</center>
<hr><center>nginx/1.10.3</center>
<hr><center>nginx/1.10.3</center>
<hr><center>nginx/1.10.3</center>
<hr><center>nginx/1.10.3</center>
<hr><center>nginx/1.10.3</center>
<hr><center>nginx/1.10.3</center>
<hr><center>nginx/1.10.3</center>
<hr><center>nginx/1.10.3</center>
<hr><center>nginx/1.10.3</center>
<hr><center>nginx/1.10.3</center>
<hr><center>nginx/1.11.13</center>
<hr><center>nginx/1.11.13</center>
<hr><center>nginx/1.11.13</center>
<hr><center>nginx/1.11.13</center>
<hr><center>nginx/1.11.13</center>
<hr><center>nginx/1.11.13</center>
<hr><center>nginx/1.11.13</center>
<hr><center>nginx/1.11.13</center>
<hr><center>nginx/1.11.13</center>
<hr><center>nginx/1.11.13</center>
<hr><center>nginx/1.11.13</center>
```

6. For cleanup, stop the cURL command with *Ctrl + C* and exit from the pod by writing exit. The pod will be deleted by Kubernetes upon exit. Run the following command:

```
kubectl delete -f rolling.yaml
```

 You can find the `rolling.yaml` file at: `https://goo.gl/eo8cJw`.

Blue/Green Strategy

The blue/green strategy is the idea of having two active production environments, namely blue and green. The blue environment is active and serving requests. The green environment has the new version, and it is being tested for the update. When the tests are completed successfully, the load balancer is switched from blue to green instances. In Kubernetes, blue/green deployment is handled by installing both versions and then changing the configuration of a service or resource.

1. The main steps of the blue/green strategy can be defined as follows:Both the **V1** and **V2** instances are deployed, and the load balancer is configured for **V1** instances:

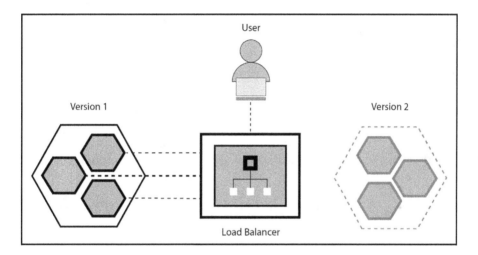

2. After testing, the load balancer is configured for route **V2** instances:

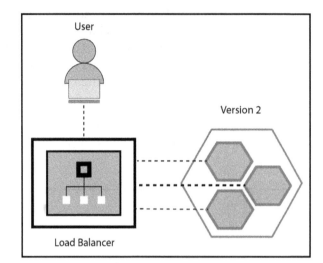

Advantages of the blue/green strategy include instant rollout and rollback, and no version mismatch during the update. On the other hand, a drawback of this strategy is that you are using double the resources since two environments are maintained. It should be noted that exhaustive end-to-end testing of applications should be handled before using this strategy.

Deploying an Application Using the Blue/Green Strategy

You are running a high-available application on Kubernetes that needs a deployment strategy to handle updates. This application, for example, a mortgage calculation engine API, has different versions, which result in different calculation results. Therefore, the client requires extensive testing before release and instant switches between the versions. We'll run an application with blue/green strategy so that both versions are running, and Kubernetes service handles instant switch of version. We'll run an application with blue/green strategy so that both versions are running, and Kubernetes service handles instant switch of version. Let's begin by performing the following steps:

1. Create both versions of the deployment and the common service with the following command:

```
kubectl apply -f blue-green.yaml
```

2. Check that both versions are deployed on the cluster with the following command:

```
kubectl get pods
```

You should see the following output:

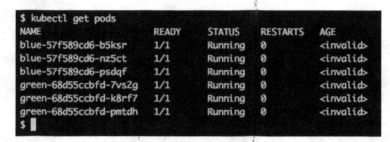

```
$ kubectl get pods
NAME                       READY   STATUS    RESTARTS   AGE
blue-57f589cd6-b5ksr       1/1     Running   0          <invalid>
blue-57f589cd6-nz5ct       1/1     Running   0          <invalid>
blue-57f589cd6-psdqf       1/1     Running   0          <invalid>
green-68d55ccbfd-7vs2g     1/1     Running   0          <invalid>
green-68d55ccbfd-k8rf7     1/1     Running   0          <invalid>
green-68d55ccbfd-pmtdh     1/1     Running   0          <invalid>
$
```

3. In a separate terminal, start a cURL instance in the Kubernetes cluster:

```
kubectl run curl --image=tutum/curl --rm -it
```

4. When the command prompt is ready, watch for the version of the deployment by using an HTTP request:

```
while sleep 0.5; do curl -s http://blue-green/version | grep nginx;
done
```

5. Update the service to route traffic to the new version with the following command:

```
kubectl patch service blue-green -p
'{"spec":{"selector":{"version":"1.11"}}}'
```

6. In the terminal that we opened in Step 3, we should see the Kubernetes service handling an instant change of versions without any interruption:

```
root@curl-54988bf969-z6xjz:/# while sleep 0.5; do curl -s http://rolling/version | grep nginx; done
<hr><center>nginx/1.10.3</center>
<hr><center>nginx/1.10.3</center>
<hr><center>nginx/1.10.3</center>
<hr><center>nginx/1.10.3</center>
<hr><center>nginx/1.10.3</center>
<hr><center>nginx/1.10.3</center>
<hr><center>nginx/1.10.3</center>
<hr><center>nginx/1.10.3</center>
<hr><center>nginx/1.10.3</center>
<hr><center>nginx/1.11.13</center>
<hr><center>nginx/1.11.13</center>
<hr><center>nginx/1.11.13</center>
<hr><center>nginx/1.11.13</center>
<hr><center>nginx/1.10.3</center>
<hr><center>nginx/1.10.3</center>
<hr><center>nginx/1.11.13</center>
<hr><center>nginx/1.11.13</center>
<hr><center>nginx/1.10.3</center>
<hr><center>nginx/1.11.13</center>
<hr><center>nginx/1.11.13</center>
<hr><center>nginx/1.11.13</center>
<hr><center>nginx/1.11.13</center>
<hr><center>nginx/1.11.13</center>
<hr><center>nginx/1.11.13</center>
<hr><center>nginx/1.11.13</center>
<hr><center>nginx/1.11.13</center>
<hr><center>nginx/1.11.13</center>
```

7. For cleanup, stop the cURL command with *Ctrl* + *C* and exit from the pod by writing exit. The pod will be deleted by Kubernetes upon exit. Run the following command:

```
kubectl delete -f blue-green.yaml
```

A/B Testing Strategy

The A/B testing strategy is based on the idea of consumer separation and providing different subsets of functionalities. A/B testing allows you to run multiple variants of functionality in parallel. With the analytics of user behavior, users can be routed to a more appropriate version. The following is a sample list of conditions that can be used in order to scatter traffic:

- Cookies
- Location
- Technology, such as the browser, screen size, and mobility
- Language

In the following image, both versions are installed, and users are routed based on their technology characteristics, that is, mobile or desktop:

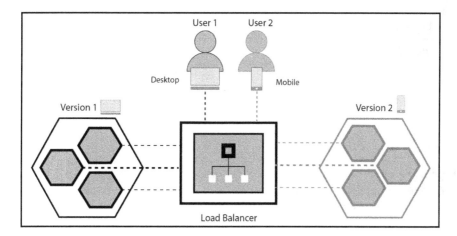

The main advantage of the A/B testing strategy is that you have full control over traffic. However, distributing the traffic requires an intelligent load balancer other than the regular Kubernetes services. Some of the popular applications for this are as follows:

- Linkerd
- Traefik
- NGINX
- HAProxy
- Istio

Linkerd, Traefik, NGINX, and HAProxy are data plane applications that focus on forwarding and observing network packages between service instances. On the other hand, Istio is a control plane application that focuses on the configuration and management of proxies that route traffic.

Deployment Strategies Summary

Before choosing a deployment strategy, it should be taken into consideration that there is no silver bullet to solve all production environment requirements. Therefore, it is crucial to check and compare the advantages and disadvantages of strategies and choose the most appropriate one:

Strategy	Zero downtime	Real traffic testing	Targeted users
Recreate	No	No	No
Rolling update	Yes	No	No
Blue/Green	Yes	No	No
A/B testing	Yes	Yes	Yes

Summary

In this chapter, Kubernetes design patterns, which are the best practices for cloud-native applications, were presented. Firstly, the idea of design patterns was explained by their usage and classification. Following that, Kubernetes design patterns were presented, followed by some in-class activities. Kubernetes, being the prominent framework for cloud-native applications, has the flexibility and coverage to meet every business requirement. However, knowing how to use Kubernetes resources compellingly is crucial. This is exactly what we covered in this chapter.

Kubernetes Client Libraries

2

Kubernetes provides multiple options for creating applications with the Kubernetes API. These options include tools such as `kubectl`, `helm`, `kops`, and `kubeadm`; and client libraries, which are officially supported or community-maintained. However, it is essential that you know the capabilities and boundaries of the clients in order to create applications that interact with Kubernetes.

In this chapter, you will learn how to access the Kubernetes API directly and use Kubernetes client libraries. Firstly, direct access to the Kubernetes API will be explained, and responses from the Kubernetes API will be demonstrated. Following that, official and community-maintained libraries will be given, including detailed information and example applications. Throughout this chapter, you'll develop applications that connect to the Kubernetes API, inside and outside the cluster.

By the end of this chapter, you will be able to:

- Evaluate the Kubernetes API request and response style
- Connect to the Kubernetes API using HTTP
- Find and use official client libraries
- Write, run, and deploy client library applications
- Evaluate community-maintained client libraries for further projects

Accessing the Kubernetes API

Kubernetes consists of several loosely-coupled components, with the principal idea of managing versioned resources. Kubernetes components can be divided into two sections: the control plane and node components. The control plane consists of the API Server, Controller Managers, and Schedulers. The API Server is the core management component and has the following functionalities:

- Serves a REST API for the clients outside the cluster and Kubernetes components inside the cluster
- Creates, deletes, and updates all of the Kubernetes resources, such as pods, deployments, and services
- Stores the state of the objects in a distributed key/value store

Kubernetes API Style

The Kubernetes API is a RESTful service that requires all clients to create, read, update, and delete resources using HTTP requests, such as GET, PUT, POST, and DELETE. Client applications such as kubectl or client libraries in various programming languages implement the API response and request types. For communication, the Kubernetes API accepts and returns JSON data, just like most of the RESTful services that are available.

 Representational State Transfer (REST) is an architectural style for web applications so that they can use HTTP requests. As a convention, GET is used for reading resources, POST is used for creating resources, PUT is used for updating resources, and DELETE is used for deleting resources.

Servers that apply the RESTful API are expected to have clients without any knowledge of server structure. Likewise, the server should provide all related information for the client so that it can operate and interact with itself.

JavaScript Object Notation (JSON) is a popular and lightweight data exchange format. JSON is suitable for machine parsing and generation, and is human-readable and expressive. Although written in JavaScript, JSON is supported by multiple languages and is a crucial data type of modern asynchronous browser/server communication.

In the following section, the Kubernetes API response style will be explored by calling an API server REST endpoint.

Getting a JSON Response from the Kubernetes API

This section shows how to retrieve raw data from the Kubernetes API by using `kubectl` and analyze the data as a JSON object for the parts of the resource.

Let's begin by implementing the following steps:

1. Get the raw data with the following command:

    ```
    kubectl get --raw /api/v1/namespaces/kube-system
    ```

2. As a result, you will see a JSON response. Let's get the same command and format the output:

    ```
    kubectl get --raw /api/v1/namespaces/kube-system | python -m
    json.tool
    ```

    If Python is not locally installed, any online JSON formatter can be used by copying and pasting the output.

3. The JSON response shows the structure of a Kubernetes API resource:

    ```
    {
    "apiVersion": "v1",
    "kind": "Namespace",
    "metadata": {
        "creationTimestamp": "2018-04-15T10:21:34Z",
        "name": "kube-system",
        "resourceVersion": "81",
        "selfLink": "/api/v1/namespaces/kube-system",
        "uid": "c5db1188-4096-11e8-903d-0800273b4d24"
    },
    ```

Kubernetes API resources have `"apiVersion"` since all resources are versioned in the system. `"kind"` shows the type of the resource and `"metadata"` has all of the meta information, such as the creation timestamp, labels, or annotations. `"spec"` is the part where all properties of the resource are listed. Finally, most of the resources have a `"status"` section to show their state, errors, or messages (if any).

Accessing the Kubernetes API

The Kubernetes API server is secure, requiring all incoming connections to be authenticated. There are two common ways of connecting and securely communicating with the Kubernetes API server. The first one is by using the reverse proxy functionality of kubectl and the second one is by using the API server credentials. These approaches can be summarized as follows:

- The reverse proxy Kubernetes API with kubectl:
  - The Kubectl proxy command starts a proxy server between the localhost and the Kubernetes API server.
  - All incoming requests are forwarded to the remote Kubernetes API server port.
  - The API server identity is verified by using self-signed certificates so that no **Man-in-the-Middle** (**MITM**) attacks are is possible.
  - kubectl handles authentication to the API server. This is a recommended approach in the official Kubernetes documentation.
  - Further development is ongoing; client-side load balancing and failover features could be provided in the future.
- Provides the API server address and credentials directly:
  - The API server address and credentials are available within and outside the cluster and they can be provided as parameters.
  - This is an alternative approach and should be used as a last resort if the client application cannot work with a reversed proxy.
  - In order to protect from MITM attacks, certificates should be imported to the clients, for example, through browsers.

In the following activity, connecting to the Kubernetes API by using the `kubectl` proxy is carried out to create a new Kubernetes namespace. With this method, `kubectl` securely connects to the API server with its own credentials and creates a proxy for the applications on the local system.

Connecting to the Kubernetes API and Creating Namespaces

In this section, you are assigned the job of creating namespaces for tests by using the Kubernetes API. Tests are running outside the cluster and communicate with the Kubernetes API. In order to run tests in their own namespaces, you need to create a namespace. With the successful completion of this task, a new namespace will be created within Kubernetes by sending JSON data. Let's ensure to follow these steps before starting with our example:

- Create a proxy with kubectl and make it available to all applications on the local system
- Use JSON and cURL to communicate with the Kubernetes API
- Gather the JSON structure of the namespace resource by querying kubesystem and use it as a template

Let's begin by implementing the following steps:

1. Start the reverse proxy with the following command:

```
kubectl proxy --port=8080
```

2. In another terminal, create an HTTP request to the forwarded port:

```
curl http://localhost:8080/api/v1/namespaces/kube-system
```

The response is expected to be a JSON structure similar to the following:

```
$ curl http://localhost:8080/api/v1/namespaces/kube-system
{
  "kind": "Namespace",
  "apiVersion": "v1",
  "metadata": {
    "name": "kube-system",
    "selfLink": "/api/v1/namespaces/kube-system",
    "uid": "481b60d0-2777-11e8-94ed-025000000001",
    "resourceVersion": "12",
    "creationTimestamp": "2018-03-14T11:03:09Z"
  },
  "spec": {
    "finalizers": [
      "kubernetes"
    ]
  },
  "status": {
    "phase": "Active"
  }
}$ 
```

3. Using the response of *Step 2* as a template, create a simple namespace JSON object:

```
{
"apiVersion":"v1",
"kind":"Namespace",
"metadata":{
"name":"packt-client"
}
}
```

4. Create the new namespace by using `curl` with the payload data from *Step 3*:

```
curl -X POST http://localhost:8080/api/v1/namespaces/ \
--header "Content-Type: application/json" \
--data \
'{"apiVersion":"v1","kind":"Namespace","metadata":{"name":"packt-
client"}}'
```

As a result of this command, the newly created namespace data will be received:

```
$ curl -X POST http://localhost:8080/api/v1/namespaces/ \
> --header "Content-Type: application/json" \
> --data '{"apiVersion":"v1","kind":"Namespace","metadata":{"name":"packt-client
"}}'
{
    "kind": "Namespace",
    "apiVersion": "v1",
    "metadata": {
      "name": "packt-client",
      "selfLink": "/api/v1/namespaces/packt-client",
      "uid": "9bf51f41-4872-11e8-bc2d-025000000001",
      "resourceVersion": "1399328",
      "creationTimestamp": "2018-04-25T10:22:51Z"
    },
    "spec": {
      "finalizers": [
        "kubernetes"
      ]
    },
    "status": {
      "phase": "Active"
    }
}$
```

5. You can run the following command for cleanup:

```
kubectl delete namespace packt-client
```

Accessing the Kubernetes API inside a Cluster

Accessing the Kubernetes API outside the cluster is mostly done for operational bases where human interaction is required. In addition to outside communication, accessing the Kubernetes API inside the cluster to make requests to the API server is also possible. It enables writing applications and running them inside the cluster, which could convert operational knowledge into applications.

For all of the pods in the cluster, Kubernetes injects service accounts – they are the recommended way of authenticating to the Kubernetes API server. For each pod, the following information and credentials related to service accounts are mounted by default:

- **Service account and token**:
  `/var/run/secrets/kubernetes.io/serviceaccount/token`
- **Certificate bundle**:
  `/var/run/secrets/kubernetes.io/serviceaccount/ca.crt`
- **Namespace**:
  `/var/run/secrets/kubernetes.io/serviceaccount/namespace`

 Using this information within the cluster forms a secure way of connecting to the Kubernetes API server and making requests. The service account, which is an authentication mechanism in Kubernetes, uses signed tokens to verify requests. They are created and managed by the Kubernetes API server. For each pod running in Kubernetes, service account tokens are mounted, and they enable pods to communicate with the Kubernetes API server. Further information is available in the official documentation: `https://kubernetes.io/docs/admin/authentication`.

To Connect to the Kubernetes API inside a Cluster

In this section, we'll create a simple application to query the Kubernetes API and get the details of the kube-system namespace. However, this application should run inside the cluster and work as a Kubernetes native application. We'll query the Kubernetes API within a cluster with the injected environment variables and certificates in the pods.

Let's begin by implementing the following steps:

1. Start a cURL instance inside the cluster and wait until it is up and running:

```
kubectl run curl --image=tutum/curl --rm -it
```

2. Inside the pod, check the security credentials:

```
ls /var/run/secrets/kubernetes.io/serviceaccount/
```

You'll get the following output:

```
$ kubectl run curl --image=tutum/curl --rm -it
If you don't see a command prompt, try pressing enter.
root@curl-54988bf969-j7c7h:/#
root@curl-54988bf969-j7c7h:/# ls /var/run/secrets/kubernetes.io/serviceaccount/
ca.crt  namespace  token
root@curl-54988bf969-j7c7h:/#
```

3. Check that the Kubernetes API server has the related environment variables:

```
env | grep KUBE
```

You'll get the following output:

```
root@curl-54988bf969-j7c7h:/# env | grep KUBE
KUBERNETES_PORT_443_TCP_PORT=443
KUBERNETES_PORT=tcp://10.96.0.1:443
KUBERNETES_SERVICE_PORT=443
KUBERNETES_SERVICE_HOST=10.96.0.1
KUBERNETES_PORT_443_TCP_PROTO=tcp
KUBERNETES_SERVICE_PORT_HTTPS=443
KUBERNETES_PORT_443_TCP_ADDR=10.96.0.1
KUBERNETES_PORT_443_TCP=tcp://10.96.0.1:443
root@curl-54988bf969-j7c7h:/#
```

4. Combine all of the credentials and address information together with the following commands:

```
APISERVER=https://$KUBERNETES_SERVICE_HOST:$KUBERNETES_SERVICE_PORT
TOKEN=$(cat /var/run/secrets/kubernetes.io/serviceaccount/token)
CACERT=/var/run/secrets/kubernetes.io/serviceaccount/ca.crt
NAMESPACE=$(cat
/var/run/secrets/kubernetes.io/serviceaccount/namespace)
```

5. With the collected environment variables from *Step 4*, create and send an HTTP request by using cURL:

```
curl --header "Authorization: Bearer $TOKEN" --cacert
$CACERT $APISERVER/api/v1/namespaces/kube-system
```

By using the preceding command, a GET request will be sent to the `/api/v1/namespaces/kube-system` endpoint. In order to authenticate to the API server, a bearer token is sent as a header, and certificate authority information is provided.

As a result of this command, the requested namespace information will be retrieved from the API server:

```
root@curl-54988bf969-j7c7h:/# curl --header "Authorization: Bearer $TOKEN" --cacert $CACERT
$APISERVER/api/v1/namespaces/kube-system
{
  "kind": "Namespace",
  "apiVersion": "v1",
  "metadata": {
    "name": "kube-system",
    "selfLink": "/api/v1/namespaces/kube-system",
    "uid": "481b60d0-2777-11e8-94ed-025000000001",
    "resourceVersion": "12",
    "creationTimestamp": "2018-03-14T11:03:09Z"
  },
  "spec": {
    "finalizers": [
      "kubernetes"
    ]
  },
  "status": {
    "phase": "Active"
  }
}root@curl-54988bf969-j7c7h:/#
```

The Kubernetes API is the core management service and it is a secure RESTful service that consumes JSON. It requires all of the clients to be authenticated, and both outside and inside cluster connections are possible. In the following section, client libraries for various programming languages are presented that implement the Kubernetes API.

Official Client Libraries

Applications that consume the Kubernetes REST API should implement API calls, including request and response types. Considering the rich set of Kubernetes resources that are provided to us, developing and maintaining API implementation becomes complex. Fortunately, Kubernetes has a rich set of official client libraries that are implemented in various programming languages. Client libraries do not only handle requests and responses, but also handle authentication to the API server. Besides, most of the client libraries can discover and connect to the Kubernetes API server if it is running inside the cluster.

In this section, official Go and Python client libraries will be presented. The client repositories, documentation, how to install, and how to create simple applications that are running inside and outside the clusters will be covered.

Go Client Library

Go, which is also of en referred to as Golang, is a programming language that was created by Google in 2009. Prominent features of Go include the following:

- It is statically typed so that the compiler ensures object types and conversions are working
- It has memory safety with no development concerns
- It has garbage collection with a minimal overhead
- The structural typing of objects is based on their composition
- It has first-citizen concurrency handling with primitives such as go routines and channels

Go is a free, open source programming language that has compilers and environment tools. Go became popular within cloud-native applications because the aforementioned features are well-fitting to the requirements of scalable and reliable applications. Some of the most notable projects that use Go as their primary language are as follows:

- Docker
- Kubernetes
- Terraform
- OpenShift

- Consul
- Bitcoin Lightning Network
- InfluxDB
- CockroachDB

Repository

Kubernetes' Go client, namely client-go, is part of the Kubernetes official project, which is available at `https://github.com/kubernetes/client-go`.

It is the oldest and the most comprehensive client library. Kubernetes resource handlers of the client library are generated with the official source code generators from Kubernetes. In addition, client-go is widely used inside Kubernetes projects, such as kubectl, helm, and kops.

Documentation

The Go client repository consists of the following packages and respective focus areas:

- `kubernetes`: Clientset to access the Kubernetes API
- `discovery`: Discover APIs supported by the Kubernetes API server
- `dynamic`: Dynamic client to perform generic API access
- `transport`: Authentication and connection start
- `tools/cache`: Helpers for writing controllers

The Go client follows the official documentation style of the Go language and it is available at `https://godoc.org/k8s.io/client-go`.

Installation

In the Go language, its toolset provides the `go get` command as a standard way of downloading and installing packages with their dependencies. This command downloads the default branch and the latest changes from source control version providers. However, specific versions of the Kubernetes client are designed to work with particular versions of dependencies. Therefore, the standard `go get` command is not usable. Instead, dependency management solutions proposed for Go should be used to work with `client-go` reliably.

In other words, the required version of client-go should be decided, and then the dependency manager downloads it with the corresponding dependencies. This concept of handling dependencies is called **vendoring**. Accordingly, dependency managers collect the dependency libraries and put them in the `vendor` folder.

For a Go application that uses the `client-go` library, all related libraries and their dependencies should be collected under the vendor folder for reliable and repeatable builds.

 The Kubernetes Go client supports multiple dependency management tools, such as dep, godeps, and glide. In addition, the required steps for casual users who do not want to use any dependency management tools are provided in the official documentation of client-go: `https://github.com/kubernetes/client-go/blob/master/INSTALL.md`.

Creating Configuration

The Go client library provides the necessary functionalities to connect to the Kubernetes API server. It is easy to create the configuration so that you can communicate outside the cluster and inside the cluster. You can do so with the following code snippets:

```
// Create configuration outside the cluster config, err =
clientcmd.BuildConfigFromFlags("", kubeconfigPath)
// Create configuration inside the cluster config, err =
rest.InClusterConfig()
```

Creating Clientset

Clientset contains the clients for each groupof resources and provides access to them. With its redacted version, as shown in the following code, it can be seen that every group of resources have their clients implemented in the client library:

```
type Clientset struct {
        ...
        appsV1 *appsv1.AppsV1Client
        ...
        batchV1 *batchv1.BatchV1Client
        coreV1 *corev1.CoreV1Client
        eventsV1beta1 *eventsv1beta1.EventsV1beta1Client
        networkingV1 *networkingv1.NetworkingV1Client
```

```
        rbacV1 *rbacv1.RbacV1Client
        storageV1beta1 *storagev1beta1.StorageV1beta1Client
        storageV1 *storagev1.StorageV1Client
    }
```

Using the configuration from the previous step, clientset can be created with the following code snippet:

```
// Create clientset from configuration
clientset, err := kubernetes.NewForConfig(config)
```

Making API Calls

After creating the configuration and clientset, API calls can finally be carried out. All of the Kubernetes resources can be listed, updated, created, or deleted by using the clients in the provided clientset. Some examples are shown in the following code snippet:

```
// Request all pods from all namespaces
pods, err :=
clientset.CoreV1().Pods(v1.NamespaceAll).List(metav1.ListOptions{})
 // Get deployment packt from the default namespace
deployments, err :=
clientset.AppsV1().Deployments(v1.NamespaceDefault).Get("packt",
metav1.GetOptions{})
// Delete statefulset test from namespace packt
clientset.AppsV1().StatefulSets("packt").Delete("test",
&amp;metav1.DeleteOptions{})
```

 Code snippets are provided for the configuration, client creation, and making API calls using the Kubernetes Go client in the previous sections. The complete application code is provided in go/main.go, bringing together all of the snippets at https://goo.gl/wJBjG5.

We can note the following points in the main.go file:

- In the main function that was started at *line 19*, all of the variables are defined, and the command-line arguments are parsed at *line 30*.
- Configuration is created from kubeconfig, and as a fallback method, it is created by in-cluster methods between *lines 33* and *42*.
- Clientset is created at *line 45*.

- Between *lines 51* and *65*, an indefinite loop is defined with 10 seconds of sleep at the end of iterations.
- At every iteration of this loop, pods from all namespaces are requested at *line 53*. The response is printed to the console between *lines 58* and *62*.

In the following example, an application combining all of the code snippets in the previous sections is built and run. It shows you how to build a Go application and use it outside the cluster. Although the application seems straightforward, the flow and codebase creates a foundation for complex automation requirements.

To Use the Kubernetes Go Client outside the Cluster

In this section, we'll learn to build and run a Go application, consuming Kubernetes Go client and connecting the application outside the cluster. Go applications are built by using go toolset commands such as go build. However, this requires the installation of Go locally. In this example, we will use the official Docker image of the Go language without any installation on the local machine:

1. Create a cross-platform build using the official Docker container by using the following command:

```
cd go
make build
```

2. Start the application using the executable we created in *Step 1* and the kubeconfig file location:

```
./client --kubeconfig=$HOME/.kube/config
```

You will see the following output:

```
$ ./go-client --kubeconfig=/Users/i313226/.kube/config
There are 7 pods in the cluster:
kube-system/heapster-9lztd
kube-system/influxdb-grafana-4csdg
kube-system/kube-addon-manager-minikube
kube-system/kube-dns-54cccfbdf8-sbzkn
kube-system/kubernetes-dashboard-77d8b98585-4tsqd
kube-system/storage-provisioner
kube-system/tiller-deploy-5f64c57bcb-8rmgz
```

Activity: Using the Kubernetes Go Client inside the Cluster

Scenario

You are assigned the task of deploying a Go application that lists all of the pods in Kubernetes. Besides this, the application will run inside the cluster and receive information about its cluster.

Aim

To run an application that consumes the Go client library inside the Kubernetes cluster.

Prerequisites

1. Use the Docker image `onuryilmaz/k8s-client-example:go` image, which contains the executable from the previous example.
2. Deploy the application and check the logs to see whether it is working as expected.

Steps for Completion

1. Create a deployment with the Docker image of the example client from the previous example.
2. Wait until the pod is running.
3. Get the logs of the deployment pod.

   With this command, the logs of the pod are retrieved with a subcommand. In the subcommand, all pods are retrieved with the selector label of `run` equal to `go-client`, and the name of the first pod is gathered. Logs should indicate the client itself, in addition to other pods in the cluster:

```
$ kubectl logs $(kubectl get pods --selector run=go-client   -o jsonpath="{.items[0].metadata.name}")
There are 8 pods in the cluster:
default/go-client-74b44fff9c-2brtw
kube-system/heapster-9lztd
kube-system/influxdb-grafana-4csdg
kube-system/kube-addon-manager-minikube
kube-system/kube-dns-54cccfbdf8-sbzkn
kube-system/kubernetes-dashboard-77d8b98585-4tsqd
kube-system/storage-provisioner
kube-system/tiller-deploy-5f64c57bcb-8rmgz
$
```

4. Run the following command for cleanup:

```
kubectl delete deployment go-client
```

Python Client Library

Python is a high-level and general-purpose programming language that was first released in 1990. It is one of the most popular open source programming languages, used in various areas, including machine learning, data processing, web development, and scripting. The essential feature of Python is that the language is interpreted with dynamic type checking. Python owes its popularity to its clear programming style and focus on code readability. In modern cloud-native environments, Python is mostly used for infrastructure and automation. In addition to its popularity and widespread usage, Kubernetes has an official client library that's implemented in Python.

Repository

The Kubernetes Python client is part of the official client repository and is available at `https://github.com/kubernetes-client/python`.

The Python client is an OpenAPI compliant client, which means that Swagger tools generate resource definitions. The client library is still in progress, and its capabilities should be checked from the repository before using them in production. The Python client, like every other Kubernetes client, attempts to support a set of predefined functionalities, and it is classified as "Silver" according to its coverage.

The OpenAPI is a specification for describing RESTful APIs. Using the OpenAPI specification, it is possible to create an implementation for clients and services, including all of the corresponding operations.

Swagger is the tooling ecosystem for developing APIs, which is defined in OpenAPI. Swagger provides both open source and commercial tools to create applications for the provided specification.

Installation

There are two ways of installing the client library so that you can create a development environment. The first way is to download the source code and build:

```
$ git clone --recursive https://github.com/kubernetes-client/
python.git
$ cd python
$ python setup.py install
```

The second way is to download the package from the Python Package Index by using a package manager such as `pip`:

```
$ pip install kubernetes
```

Client Usage

In the previous section, a Go application that lists all the pods was developed. The same functionality as the previous application is performed in Python in this section. With the clean code and readability philosophy of Python, the same functionality is handled in around ten lines of code, as follows:

```
from kubernetes import client, config
import time
config.load_incluster_config()
v1 = client.CoreV1Api()
while True:
        ret = v1.list_pod_for_all_namespaces(watch=False)
        print('There are {:d} pods in the
cluster:'.format(len(ret.items)))
        for i in ret.items:
                print('{:s}/{:s}'.format((i.metadata.namespace,
i.metadata.name))
        time.sleep(10)
```

These are the critical points to mention about the preceding code snippet:

- In *line 3*, the in-cluster configuration, and in *line 5*, the client for the `corev1` API are created.
- Starting in *line 8*, an infinite loop starts with a sleep of 10 seconds at each iteration.
- In *line 9*, all pods are requested from the `v1` client and the response is parsed and written to the console.

Packaging

The Python application should run inside a container, like all services running on Kubernetes. Thus, the client library defined in this section is packaged with the following Dockerfile. This container definition enables the application to run its isolated environment with its dependencies:

```
FROM python:3
RUN pip install kubernetes
ADD . /client.py
CMD ["python", "./client.py"]
```

 Please refer to the complete code at: `https://goo.gl/z78SKr`.

The following are remarks about the preceding code:

- The container has the basis of Python supporting version 3.
- The Kubernetes Python client library is installed using `pip` in *line 3*.
- The client application is copied into the container in *line 5* and started in *line 7*.

In the following section, the code snippets presented for Python are utilized to work in a Kubernetes cluster. The complete code is packaged as a Docker container with its dependencies. With this container, the application is deployed to Kubernetes in an isolated way, which follows a microservice architecture.

Using the Kubernetes Python Client inside the Cluster

In this section, we'll deploy a Python application that lists all of the pods and consumes the Python client library inside Kubernetes. Besides this, the application will run inside the cluster and gather information about its cluster.

Before starting with the implementation, we need to use the Docker image `onuryilmaz/k8s-client-example:python`, which was built using the Dockerfile in the last section. We also need to deploy the application as a deployment and check the logs to see whether it is working as expected. Let's begin by implementing the following steps:

1. Create a deployment with the Docker image of the example client:

   ```
   kubectl run python-client -it --image=onuryilmaz/k8sclient-
   example:python
   ```

   With this command, a deployment with the name python-client will be created with the Docker image `onuryilmaz/k8s-client-example:python` in an interactive mode so that logs will be printed to the console.

   Logs should indicate the client itself, in addition to other pods in the cluster:

   ```
   $ kubectl run python-client -it --image=onuryilmaz/k8s-client-example:python

   If you don't see a command prompt, try pressing enter.

   There are 7 pods in the cluster:
   default/python-client-69bc9868b7-gdmm8
   kube-system/heapster-9lztd
   kube-system/influxdb-grafana-4csdg
   kube-system/kube-addon-manager-minikube
   kube-system/kube-dns-54cccfbdf8-sbzkn
   kube-system/kubernetes-dashboard-77d8b98585-4tsqd
   kube-system/storage-provisioner
   ```

2. Run the following command for cleanup:

   ```
   kubectl delete deployment python-client
   ```

Other Official Client Libraries

In this chapter, two official Kubernetes client libraries have been covered:

- **Go**: This is a statically typed compiler-based language
- **Python**: This is a dynamically typed and interpreted language

Official client libraries also include some additional programming languages:

- **Java**: https://github.com/kubernetes-client/java
- **.NET**: https://github.com/kubernetes-client/csharp
- **JavaScript**: https://github.com/kubernetes-client/javascript

For the capabilities and hurdles of these libraries, you should check their corresponding repositories since they are all still in the development phase.

Community-Maintained Client Libraries

Kubernetes has an active and collaborative open source community, which has also increased its popularity. There are around 20 community-maintained client libraries that are listed in the Kubernetes documentation, which cover the following languages:

- Clojure
- Go
- Java
- Lisp
- Node.js
- Perl
- PHP
- Python
- Ruby
- Scala
- dotNet
- Elixir

There are some critical points to consider before using a community-maintained client library:

- **Aim of the library**: It is crucial to consider the aim of the development team and library. Although it seems not directly related to the software itself, it affects how the client library is developed. For instance, some libraries focus on simplicity and compromise on capability coverage. If the vision of your application and the client library don't match, it would be difficult to maintain the application in the long run.

- **Version and support**: Official libraries support specific Kubernetes API versions and maintain a compatibility matrix. It is critical to work with the client libraries that work with your Kubernetes cluster, and it is also essential to get support for future Kubernetes versions. A community-maintained client library could be very suitable today but depreciate in six months if not supported.
- **Community interest**: If the considered client library is open source, its community should be alive and interested in making the library better. It is very common to see some libraries start very well but not be maintained due to a missing community. It is not advised to use a client library with old issues without any comments or pull requests that are not reviewed for a very long time.

Summary

In this chapter, Kubernetes API access and client libraries were discussed. Although there are various tools for communicating with Kubernetes, knowing the Kubernetes API itself and the client libraries is crucial for creating game-changing automation and orchestration tasks.

Firstly, the Kubernetes API style and how to connect using HTTP clients was presented. Following that, the client libraries of Kubernetes were covered, and we focused on two official client libraries. For both Go and Python, how to install, write code, package, and deploy this code into cluster steps was done with demonstrations and activities.

Finally, community-maintained libraries for different language preferences or custom requirements were shown. With the knowledge and hands-on experience of Kubernetes client libraries, higher levels of automation and extending Kubernetes is possible. In the following chapter, the best practices covered in the first chapter and the client libraries included in this chapter are gathered together to create applications that extend Kubernetes.

3
Kubernetes Extensions

Kubernetes is highly customizable and extensible so that any segment of the system can be configured comprehensively and extended with new features. Extension points of Kubernetes do not focus on low-level configuration of the built-in resources, such as pods or stateful sets. However, extending Kubernetes means extending the operations of Kubernetes itself. These extension points enable many practices, including creating new Kubernetes resources, automating Kubernetes and human interactions, and intervening with the creation or editing of resources and their scheduling mechanisms.

In this chapter, extension points and patterns will be presented, and the most common and essential extension points will be covered. Firstly, the Kubernetes API will be enhanced, and human knowledge will be converted into the automation of Kubernetes operators. Secondly, the control access mechanisms of Kubernetes will be extended with webhooks and initializers. Finally, the default scheduler of Kubernetes will be configured with highly customizable options. How to develop and deploy a custom scheduler will also be demonstrated. Throughout these chapters, you should be able to implement and deploy extensions by creating applications that consume the Kubernetes API.

Kubernetes Extension Points

Kubernetes itself and its built-in resources are highly configurable so that any modern cloud-native application can be configured to run on the cloud environment. When it comes to adding new capabilities, converting human knowledge into code and automating more, the Kubernetes extension comes to the rescue. Fortunately, to extend the capabilities of Kubernetes, users do not need to download the source code, make changes, build and deploy the complete system. With its modularity, the extension points of Kubernetes are already defined and ready to use.

Kubernetes extension points focus on the current functionalities of Kubernetes and its environment. Built-in components and how to extend Kubernetes are summarized in the following categories:

- **Kubernetes clients**: It is possible to extend client applications such as `kubectl` by writing `kubectl` plugins. These extensions will help you use `kubectl` with less human interaction, such as choosing a Kubernetes cluster context automatically. Likewise, generated clients with the OpenAPI specifications can extend client libraries such as `client-go`. With these generated clients, you can programmatically use the Kubernetes API in custom applications.
- **Kubernetes API types**: Kubernetes API resources such as pods, deployments, and many more are highly configurable, but it is also possible to add new resources called custom resources.
- **Kubernetes API controllers**: The control plane of Kubernetes, which includes the Kubernetes API server, handles all operations, such as automatic scaling or self-healing; however, it is also possible to develop custom controllers.
- **Access controllers**: The access control mechanism that handles authentication, authorization, and admission controllers can be extended by connecting to webhook servers or intervening with initializers.
- **Scheduling**: `kube-scheduler` already handles the scheduling of pods to the nodes; however, it is also possible to create custom schedulers and deploy them to the clusters.
- **Infrastructure**: The infrastructure part of Kubernetes is standardized, regarding the server, network, and storage with the **Container Runtime Interface (CRI)**, **Container Network Interface (CNI)**, and **Container Storage Interface (CSI)**. The implementation, of these interfaces provide ways of extending the infrastructure of the underlying Kubernetes clusters.

I have put the preceding categories into the following table for ease of use:

Category	Provided by Kubernetes	Extensions
Clients	kubectl	kubectl plugin
	client-go	Client generator
API types	Pod, deployment, and so on	Custom Resource Definitions
API controllers	kube-apiserver	Custom Controller
Access controllers	Authentication, authorization, and admission controller	Webhooks and initializers
Scheduling	kube-scheduler	Custom scheduler
Infrastructure	Server, network, and storage	Container Runtime Interface
		Container Network Interface
		Container Storage Interface

Extending Kubernetes Clients

Kubernetes client applications and libraries are the main entry points for accessing the Kubernetes API. With these applications and libraries, it is possible to automate and extend Kubernetes operations.

For the official Kubernetes client applications, `kubectl` can be extended by writing plugin applications. Some of the most popular plugins enhance the capabilities of `kubectl`:

- It switches the Kubernetes cluster context automatically
- It calculates and displays the uptime information of pods
- It connects via SSH into a container with a specific user

Official Kubernetes code generators can generate official Kubernetes client libraries and Kubernetes server codes. These generators create the required source code for internal versioned types, clients informers, and protobuf codecs.

With the extension points on client applications and libraries, it is possible to enhance operations that interact with Kubernetes. If your custom requirements need more than the capabilities of `kubectl` or client libraries, Kubernetes provides extension points for customization.

Extending the Kubernetes API

Kubernetes already has a rich set of resources, starting from pods as building blocks to higher-level resources such as stateful sets and deployments. Modern cloud-native applications can be deployed in terms of Kubernetes resources and their high-level configuration options. However, they are not sufficient when human expertise and operations are required. Kubernetes enables extending its own API with new resources and operates them as Kubernetes-native objects with the following features:

- **RESTful API**: New resources are directly included in the RESTful API so that they are accessible with their special endpoints.
- **Authentication and authorization**: All requests for new resources go through the steps of authentication and authorization, like native requests.
- **OpenAPI discovery**: New resources can be discovered and integrated into OpenAPI specifications.
- **Client libraries**: Client libraries such as `kubectl` or `client-go` can be used to interact with new resources.

Two major steps are involved when extending the Kubernetes API:

- Create a new Kubernetes resource to introduce the new API types
- Control and automate operations to implement custom logic as an additional API controller

Custom Resource Definitions

In Kubernetes, all of the resources have their REST endpoints in the Kubernetes API server. REST endpoints enable operations for specif c objects, such as pods, by using `/api/v1/namespaces/default/pods`. Custom resources are the extensions of the Kubernetes API that can be dynamically added or removed during runtime. They enable users of the cluster to operate on extended resources.

Custom resources are defined in **Custom Resource Definition** (**CRD**) objects. Using the built-in Kubernetes resources, namely CRDs, it is possible to add new Kubernetes API endpoints by using the Kubernetes API itself.

In the following section, a new custom resource will be created for the requirements that typically require human interaction inside Kubernetes.

Creating and Deploying Custom Resource Definitions

Consider, a client wants to watch weather reports in a scalable cloud-native way in Kubernetes. We are expected to extend the Kubernetes API so that the client and further future applications natively use weather report resources. We want to create CustomResourceDefinitions and deploy them to the cluster to check their effects, and use newly defined resources to create extended objects.

 You can find the crd.yaml file at: https://goo.gl/ovwFX1.

Let's begin by implementing the following steps:

1. Deploy the custom resource definition with kubectl with the following command:

```
kubectl apply -f k8s-operator-example/deploy/crd.yaml
```

Custom resource definitions are Kubernetes resources that enable the dynamic registration of new custom resources. An example custom resource for WeatherReport can be defined as in the k8s-operator-example/deploy/crd.yaml file, which is shown as follows:

```
apiVersion: apiextensions.k8s.io/v1beta1
kind: CustomResourceDefinition
metadata:
    name: weatherreports.k8s.packt.com
spec:
    group: k8s.packt.com
    names:
        kind: WeatherReport
        listKind: WeatherReportList
         plural: weatherreports
```

```
                    singular: weatherreport
         scope: Namespaced
         version: v1
```

Like all other Kubernetes resources, CRD has API version, kind, metadata, and specification groups. In addition, the specification of CRD includes the definition for the new custom resource. For `WeatherReport`, a REST endpoint will be created under `k8s.packt.com` with the version of `v1`, and their plural and singular forms will be used within clients.

2. Check the custom resources deployed to the cluster with the following command:

```
kubectl get crd
```

You will get the following output:

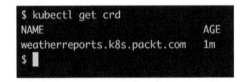

As shown in the preceding screenshot, the weather report CRD is defined with the plural name and group name.

3. Check the REST endpoints of the API server for new custom resources:

```
kubectl proxy &
curl -s localhost:8001 |grep packt
```

You will get the following output:

```
$ curl -s localhost:8001 |grep packt
    "/apis/k8s.packt.com",
    "/apis/k8s.packt.com/v1",
$ 
```

New endpoints are created, which shows that the Kubernetes API server is already extended to work with our new custom resource, `weatherreports`.

4. Check the weather report instances from Kubernetes clients such as `kubectl`:

```
kubectl get weatherreports
```

You will get the following output:

```
$ kubectl get weatherreports
No resources found.
$
```

Although the output of `No resources found` looks like an indication of an error, it shows us that there are no live instances of the `weatherreports` resource as expected. It shows us that, without any further configuration other than creating a `CustomResourceDefinition`, the Kubernetes API server is extended with new endpoints and clients are ready to work with the new custom resource.

After defining the custom resource, it is now possible to create, update, and delete resources with the `WeatherReport`. An example of `WeatherReport` can be defined, as in the `k8s-operator-example/deploy/cr.yaml` file:

```yaml
apiVersion: "k8s.packt.com/v1"
kind: WeatherReport
metadata:
    name: amsterdam-daily
spec:
    city: Amsterdam
    days: 1
```

 You can find the `cr.yaml` file at: `https://goo.gl/4A3VD2`.

The `WeatherReport` resource has the same structure, with built-in resources and consists of API version, kind, metadata, and specification. In this example, the specif cation indicates that this resource is for the weather report for `Amsterdam` city and for the last 1 day.

5. Deploy the weather report example with the following command:

```
kubectl apply -f k8s-operator-example/deploy/cr.yaml
```

6. Check for the newly created weather reports with the following command:

```
kubectl get weatherreports
```

You'll see the following output:

```
$ kubectl get weatherreports
NAME              AGE
amsterdam-daily   11s
$
```

7. Use the following commands for cleaning up:

```
kubectl delete -f k8s-operator-example/deploy/cr.yaml
kubectl delete -f k8s-operator-example/deploy/crd.yaml
```

Custom Controllers

In the previous section and exercise, we were shown that custom resources enable us to extend the Kubernetes API. However, there is also a need for taking actions against custom resources and automating the tasks. In other words, who will create the weather report and collect the results when a new `weatherreport` resource is created? The answer to this question is a custom controller in Kubernetes, which are also known as **operators**.

With the built-in Kubernetes resources, it is possible to deploy, scale, and manage stateless web applications, mobile backends, and API services easily. When it comes to the stateful applications where additional operations are required, such as initialization, storage, backup, and monitoring, domain knowledge and human expertise is needed.

A custom controller, also known as an operator, is an application where domain knowledge and human expertise is converted into code. Operators work with custom resources and take the required actions when custom resources are created, updated, or deleted. The primary tasks of operators can be divided into three sections, **Observe**, **Analyze**, and **Act**, as shown in the following diagram:

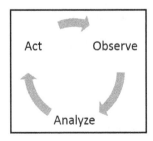

The stages are explained as follows:

- **Observe**: Watches for changes on custom resources and related built-in resources such as pods.
- **Analyze**: Makes an analysis of observed changes and decides on which actions to take.
- **Act**: Takes actions based on the analysis and requirements and continues observing for changes.

For the weather report example, the operator pattern is expected to work as follows:

- **Observe**: Wait for weather report resource creation, update, and deletion.
- **Analyze**:
  - If a new report is requested, create a pod to gather weather report results and update weather report resources.
  - If the weather report is updated, update the pod to gather new weather report results.
  - If the weather report is deleted, delete the corresponding pod.
- **Act**: Take the actions from the **Analyze** step on the cluster and continue watching with **Observe**.

Operators are already being utilized in the Kubernetes environment since they enable complex applications to run on the cloud with minimum human interaction. Storage providers (Rook), database applications (MySQL, CouchDB, PostgreSQL), big data solutions (Spark), distributed key/value stores (Consul, etcd), and many more modern cloud-native applications are installed on Kubernetes by their official operators.

Operator Development

Operators are native Kubernetes applications, and they extensively interact with the Kubernetes API. Therefore, being compliant with the Kubernetes API and converting domain expertise into software with a straightforward approach is critical for operator development. With these considerations, there are two paths for developing operators, as explained in the following sections.

Kubernetes Sample Controller

In the official Kubernetes repository, a sample controller that implements watching custom resources is maintained. This repository demonstrates how to register new custom resources and how to perform basic operations on the new resource, such as creating, updating, or listing. In addition, controller logic is also implemented to show how to take actions. Repository and interaction with the Kubernetes API is a complete approach, which shows you how to create a Kubernetes like custom controller.

Operator Framework

The Operator Framework was announced at KubeCon 2018 as an open source toolkit for managing Kubernetes native applications. The Operator SDK is a part of this framework, and it simplifies operator development by providing higher level API abstractions and code generation. The Operator Framework and its environment toolset is open source and community maintained with the control of CoreOS.

In this chapter, the Operator SDK from the Operator Framework has been selected to be used since SDK abstracts many low-level operations such as work queues, handler registrations, and informer management. With these abstractions, it is easier to handle **Observe** and **Act** parts with the packages from the SDK so that we can focus on the **Analyze** part.

In the following section, the complete life cycle of operator development is covered with the following main steps:

- **Create an operator project**: For the `WeatherReport` custom resource, an operator project in the Go language is created by using the Operator Framework SDK CLI.
- **Define custom resource specification**: The specification of the `WeatherReport` custom resource is defined in Go.
- **Implement handler logic**: The manual operations needed for weather report collection are implemented in Go.
- **Build operator**: The operator project is built using the Operator Framework SDK CLI.
- **Deploy operator**: The operator is deployed to the cluster, and it is tested by creating custom resources.

Creating and Deploying the Kubernetes Operator

A client wants to automate the operations of the weather report collection. They are currently connecting to third-party data providers and retrieving the results. In addition, they want to use cloud-native Kubernetes solutions in their clusters.

We are expected to automate the operations of weather report data collection by implementing a Kubernetes operator.

We'll create a Kubernetes operator by using the Operator Framework SDK and utilize it by creating a custom resource, custom controller logic, and finally, deploying into the cluster. Let's begin by implementing the following steps:

1. Create the operator project using the Operator Framework SDK tools with the following command:

```
operator-sdk new k8s-operator-example --api-version=k8s.
packt.com/v1 --kind=WeatherReport
```

This command creates a completely new Kubernetes operator project with the name `k8s-operator-example` and watches for the changes of the `WeatherReport` custom resource, which is defined under `k8s.packt.com/v1`. The generated operator project is available under the `k8s-operator-example` folder.

2. A custom resource definition has already been generated in the `deploy/crd.yaml` file. However, the specification of the custom resource is left empty so that it can be filled by the developer. Specifications and statuses of the custom resources are coded in Go, as shown in `pkg/apis/k8s/v1/types.go`:

```go
type WeatherReport struct {
            metav1.TypeMeta 'json:",inline"'
            metav1.ObjectMeta 'json:"metadata"'
            Spec WeatherReportSpec
'json:"spec"'
            Status WeatherReportStatus
'json:"status,omitempty"'
}
type WeatherReportSpec struct {
            City string 'json:"city"'
            Days int 'json:"days"'
}
```

You can refer to the complete code at: https://goo.gl/PSyf25.

In the preceding code snippet, WeatherReport consists of metadata, spec, and status, just like any built-in Kubernetes resource. WeatherReportSpec includes the configuration, which is City and Days in our example.WeatherReportStatus includes State and Pod to keep track of the status and the created pod for the weather report collection.

3. One of the most critical parts of the operator is the handler logic, where domain expertise and knowledge is converted into code. In this example activity, when a new WeatherReport object is created, we will publish a pod that queries the weather service and writes the result to the console output. All of these steps are coded in the pkg/stub/handler.go file as follows:

```
func (h *Handler) Handle(ctx types.Context, event types.Event)
error {
    switch o := event.Object.(type) {
        case *apiv1.WeatherReport:
            if o.Status.State == "" {
                weatherPod := weatherReportPod(o)
                err := action.Create(weatherPod)
                if err != nil && !errors.IsAlreadyExists(err) {
                    logrus.Errorf("Failed to create weather report
pod : %v", err)
```

You can refer the complete code at: https://goo.gl/uxW4jv.

In the Handle function, events carrying objects are processed. This handler function is called from the informers watching for the changes on the registered objects. If the object is WeatherReport and its status is empty, a new weather report pod is created, and the status is updated with the results.

4. Build the complete project as a Docker container with the Operator SDK and toolset:

```
operator-sdk build <DOCKER_IMAGE:DOCKER_TAG>
```

The resulting Docker container is pushed to Docker Hub as `onuryilmaz/k8s-operator-example` for further usage in the cluster.

5. Deploy the operator into the cluster with the following commands:

```
kubectl create -f deploy/crd.yaml
kubectl create -f deploy/operator.yaml
```

With the successful deployment of the operator, logs could be checked as follows:

```
kubectl logs -l name=k8s-operator-example
```

The output is as follows:

```
$ kubectl logs -l name=k8s-operator-example
time="2018-05-31T13:49:28Z" level=info msg="Go Version: go1.8"
time="2018-05-31T13:49:28Z" level=info msg="Go OS/Arch: linux/amd64"
time="2018-05-31T13:49:28Z" level=info msg="operator-sdk Version: 0.0.5"
time="2018-05-31T13:49:28Z" level=info msg="starting weatherreports controller"
$ 
```

6. After deploying the custom resource definition and the custom controller, it is time to create some resources and collect the results. Create a new `WeatherReport` instance as follows:

```
kubectl create -f deploy/cr.yaml
```

With its successful creation, the status of the `WeatherReport` can be checked:

```
kubectl describe weatherreport amsterdam-daily
```

You will see the following output:

```
$ kubectl describe weatherreport amsterdam-daily
Name:           amsterdam-daily
Namespace:      default
Labels:         <none>
Annotations:    <none>
API Version:    k8s.packt.com/v1
Kind:           WeatherReport
Metadata:
  Cluster Name:
  Creation Timestamp:  2018-05-31T14:20:28Z
  Generation:          0
  Resource Version:    2889201
  Self Link:           /apis/k8s.packt.com/v1/namespaces/default/weatherreports/amsterdam-daily
  UID:                 c48748ea-64dd-11e8-8ed2-025000000001
Spec:
  City:  Amsterdam
  Days:  1
Status:
  Pod:    weather-report-259735700
  State:  Started
Events:   <none>
$
```

7. Since the operator created a pod for the new weather report, we should see it in action and collect the results:

```
kubectl get pods
```

You'll see the following result:

```
$ kubectl get pods
NAME          READY    STATUS     RESTARTS   AGE
nginx         1/1      Running    0          44s
scheduler     1/1      Running    0          17s
$
```

8. Get the result of the weather report with the following command:

```
kubectl logs $(kubectl get weatherreport amsterdam-daily -o
jsonpath={.status.pod})
```

You'll see the following output:

```
$ kubectl logs $(kubectl get weatherreport amsterdam-daily -o jsonpath={.status.pod})
Weather report: Amsterdam, Netherlands

     \  /       Partly cloudy
   _ /"".-.     21 °C
     \_(   ).   ↘ 19 km/h
     /(___(__)  10 km
                0.0 mm
$ █
```

9. Clean up with the following command:

```
kubectl delete -f deploy/cr.yaml
kubectl delete -f deploy/operator.yaml
kubectl delete -f deploy/crd.yaml
```

Kubernetes Dynamic Admission Control

The Kubernetes API server is responsible for every request. The extension point in the request life cycle in the API server is for dynamic admission control. The admission controller is one of the most important stages of the request life cycle, since it intercepts and checks whether a request should be approved or not.

For every API request, first of all, the requester is checked by authentication and authorization. Afterward, admission controllers are run and decide to approve or reject the request. Finally, validation steps are carried out, and the resulting objects are stored:

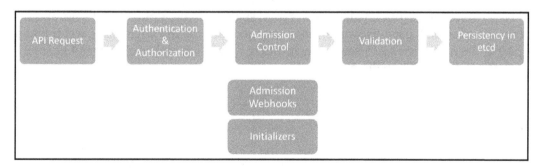

Life cycle of a Kubernetes API request

The *dynamic* part of admission control comes from the fact that they can be dynamically added, removed, or updated during the runtime of Kubernetes clusters. In addition to the built-in admission controllers, there are ways of extending admission controllers:

- Image policy webhooks for restricting the images in the cluster
- Admission webhooks for approving or rejecting the creation or updates
- Initializers for modifying objects prior to their creation

Admission Webhooks

Admission webhooks are extension points that can receive admission requests by the API server and then return accept or reject responses. As they are webhooks, HTTP requests and responses are expected by the API server. Two types of admission webhooks are supported:

- Validating admission webhooks for rejecting or accepting CRUD requests
- Mutating admission webhooks for changing the requests to enforce custom default values

Dynamic admission webhook configurations are deployed to the cluster during runtime as `MutatingWebhookConfiguration` or `ValidatingWebhookConfiguration` objects. When an API request is received, the API server creates the necessary controls during the admission webhooks stage. If there are webhook configurations defined for the request, the admission controller sends a request to the specified servers and collect the responses. If all checks are approved, validation and persistence steps continue for handling the API request.

Admission webhooks work on all request types, such as create, update, or delete, and they are robust and widely used. However, they cannot query the resources since webhooks are not part of the Kubernetes API server. In addition, admission webhooks are not generally available yet and are still in development.

Initializers

Initializers are dynamic runtime elements of the Kubernetes workflow that enable the modification of the resources before their actual creation. In other words, initializers allow developers to interfere with and make any changes to the resources, such as deployments or pods, and include custom modification logic for the Kubernetes resource life cycle.

Some possible use cases of initializers are as follows:

- Injecting a sidecar container
- Injecting a volume with certificates
- Preventing the creation of some resources that violate custom limitations

Initializers are dynamic controllers, and they are defined or removed during runtime with `InitializerConfiguration` resources. `InitializerConfiguration` combines a set of resources and initializers so that when a matching resource is created, the API server adds the corresponding initializer to the resource definition.
The list of initializers are maintained in the `metadata.initializers.pending` field. On the other hand, initializers are always watching for the new resources so that they can implement their custom logic on the objects. When *Initializer X* is in the first slot, namely `metadata.initializers.pending[0]`, *Initializer X* gets the resource and modifiers. Then, it removes itself, *Initializer X*, from the `metadata.initializers.pending` list so that the next initializer will work. When all of the initializers complete their operations, and the list is empty, the resource is released and continues the creation life cycle.

Initializers are easy to develop, and they are an extremely flexible way of extending the admission control mechanism. However, the uptime of the initializers is critical since they will block the API server. In addition, initializers are not generally available and are still in development.

Extending the Kubernetes Scheduler

Pods are the basic unit of work that are scheduled by Kubernetes to run on nodes. By default, Kubernetes has a built-in scheduler, and it tries to assign pods to the nodes evenly by ensuring that there are sufficient free resources. There are some use cases to configure and extend the scheduler behavior of Kubernetes considering the custom requirements of scalable and reliable cloud-native applications:

- Running certain pods on specialized hardware
- Co-locating some pods that include interacting services
- Dedicating some nodes to some users

Scheduler customization and extension patterns, starting from the basics to the complex, are listed as follows:

- Assigning node labels and using node selectors
- Using affinity and anti-affinity rules
- Marking nodes with taints, and pods with tolerations
- Creating and deploying custom scheduler algorithms

Node Labels

The fundamental underlying idea of scheduling is based on the labels of nodes in Kubernetes. The built-in scheduler and any custom schedulers are expected to check the specification of the nodes from their labels. With this idea, there are some integrated node labels, such as the following ones:

```
kubernetes.io/hostname
failure-domain.beta.kubernetes.io/zone
failure-domain.beta.kubernetes.io/region
beta.kubernetes.io/instance-type
beta.kubernetes.io/os
beta.kubernetes.io/arch
```

These labels and their values are assigned by the cloud providers, but do note that label values are not standardized yet. For Minikube, there is only one master node, and its labels can be checked with the following command:

```
$ kubectl get nodes --show-labels
NAME STATUS ROLES AGE VERSION LABELS
minikube Ready master 9m v1.10.0 beta.
kubernetes.io/arch=amd64, beta.kubernetes.io/os=linux, kubernetes.
io/hostname=minikube, node-role.kubernetes.io/master=
```

As highlighted, the node with the hostname `minikube` has an architecture of amd64 with an operating system, `linux`, and its `node-role` is `master`.

Node Selectors

Node selectors are the most straightforward constraints that can be used with the Kubernetes scheduler. Node selectors are part of pod specification, and they are key-value maps. The keys of the node selector are expected to match with node labels, and the values are the constraints for the scheduler.

They are included in the pod specification as follows:

```
apiVersion: v1
kind: Pod
metadata:
  name: nginx
spec:
  containers:
  - name: nginx
    image: nginx
  nodeSelector:
    beta.kubernetes.io/arch: amd64
```

With that pod definition, the Kubernetes scheduler is limited to assigning the pod `nginx` to a node with an architecture of `amd64`. If there are no nodes with the constraints, the pods will wait in a Pending state until a node that ensures the limitations join the cluster.

Node Affinity

Node affinity is a more expressive form of the nodeSelector specification, which includes two sets of constraints:

- `requiredDuringSchedulingIgnoredDuringExecution`: This set indicates the constraints that must be satisfied prior to scheduling a pod to a node. This set is similar to `nodeSelector`; however, it enables more flexible definitions.
- `preferredDuringSchedulingIgnoredDuringExecution`: This set indicates the constraints that are preferred during scheduling, but not guaranteed.

In short, the first set consists of the hard limits for the scheduler, whereas the second set consists of the soft limits. The `IgnoredDuringExecution` part indicates if labels change and constraints are not satisfied during runtime, no changes will be made by the scheduler. With these node affinity rules, it is easy to define complex rules in order to limit the scheduler. For instance, in the following pod definition with the `requiredDuringSchedulingIgnoredDuringExecution` group, pods are restricted to run only in a PowerPC environment. In addition, with the `preferredDuringSchedulingIgnoredDuringExecution` group, pods attempt to run on the nodes in availability zone A if possible:

```
apiVersion: v1
...
    requiredDuringSchedulingIgnoredDuringExecution:
...
```

```
spec:
  affinity:
        - key: kubernetes.io/arch
          operator: In
          values:
        - ppc64_le
preferredDuringSchedulingIgnoredDuringExecution:
- weight: 1
preference:
matchExpressions:
- key: failure-domain.beta.kubernetes.io/zone
  operator: In
  values:
  - availability-zone-a
```

Pod Affinity

The node affinity rules from the last section define pod and node assignment relationships. They describe a set of restrictions for pods to run on a set of nodes. With the same approach, inter-pod affinity, and anti-affinity rules, define constraints based on other pods. For instance, with the pod affinity rules, pods can be scheduled together for a limited set of nodes. Likewise, with the pod anti-affinity rules, pods can repel each other for a specific topology key, for instance, a node. For pod affinities, hard and soft limits can be defined with `requiredDuringSchedulingIgnoredDuringExecution` and `preferredDuringSchedulingIgnoredDuringExecution`.

With the following pod definition, pod affinity ensures that pods will only run on the nodes in the same availability zone, that is, pods with the `service=backend` label. In other words, affinity rules will try and ensure that our pod will be scheduled into the same availability zone, with the backend services, considering they are interacting with each other. With the pod anti-affinity, the scheduler will try not to run on the nodes that already have pods running in the `service=backend` label. In other words, if possible, they will not be scheduled to the same nodes with the backend to avoid creating a single point of failure:

```
apiVersion: v1
...
    podAffinity:
      requiredDuringSchedulingIgnoredDuringExecution:
...
spec:
  affinity:
        - key: service
          operator: In
          values:
```

```
            - backend
        topologyKey: failure-domain.beta.kubernetes.io/zone
  podAntiAffinity:
        preferredDuringSchedulingIgnoredDuringExecution:
            - key: service
              operator: In
              values:
            - backend
        topologyKey: kubernetes.io/hostname
```

Taints and Tolerations

Affinity rules define constraints for the scheduler so that they can assign pods on the nodes. On the other hand, Kubernetes provides a way of rejecting pods from the standpoint of nodes by taints and tolerations. Taints and tolerations work together so that a set of pods are not scheduled to a set of nodes. Taints are applied to the nodes to reject some pods, and tolerations allow the pod to be accepted on some nodes.

Taints tag the nodes with pod labels for "not scheduling". For instance, with the following command, no pods will be scheduled to `nodeA` unless matching tolerations are defined for key and value:

```
kubectl taint nodes nodeA key=value:NoSchedule
```

Tolerations tags the pods so that the taints are not applied to these pods. For example, with the following toleration in the pod specification, the preceding taint will not be applied:

```
apiVersion: v1
kind: Pod
metadata:
  name: with-pod-toleration
spec:
  tolerations:
  - key: "key"
    operator: "Equal"
    value: "value"
    effect: "NoSchedule"
containers:
- name: with-pod-toleration
  image: k8s.gcr.io/pause:2.0
```

Tolerations and taints work together so that nodes can be tainted with some user groups or specific labels, and tolerations can be defined in the pod definition for the following use cases:

- Dedicated nodes
- Nodes with special hardware
- Taint-based evictions for the behavior in the case of node problems

Custom Scheduler Development

The Kubernetes scheduler can be highly configured with node selectors, node affinity, pod affinity, taints, and toleration rules. In the case of custom scheduling requirements, it is also possible to develop and deploy custom schedulers in a
Kubernetes cluster. Kubernetes supports running multiple schedulers out-of-the-box. A custom scheduler in Kubernetes can be developed with any programming language. However, since it will interact extensively with the Kubernetes API, it is customary to use a programming language that has a Kubernetes client library:

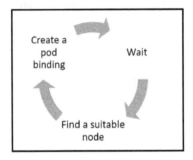

The basic workflow of the scheduler can be divided into three main consecutive stages. The scheduler waits for the pods with the specific scheduler name and no node assignment. When such a pod is found, the scheduler runs its custom algorithms to find a suitable node. Finally, the scheduler creates a binding, which is a built-in subresource of a pod in Kubernetes.

A custom scheduler in Go is implemented in the `k8s-scheduler-example/main. go` file and the basic workflow of *Wait, Find a suitable node,* and the *Create pod binding* stages are combined together in the following code snippet:

```
for {
    // Request pods from all namespaces
    pods, err :=
clientset.CoreV1().Pods(v1.NamespaceAll).List(metav1.ListOptions{})
```

```
    . . .
        // Check for pods
    for _, pod := range pods.Items {
        // If scheduler name is set and node is not assigned
        if pod.Spec.SchedulerName == *schedulerName && pod.Spec.
        NodeName == "" {
            // Schedule the pod to a random node
            err := schedule(pod.Name, randomNode(), pod.Namespace)
            . . .
        }
    }
    . . .
}
```

The `schedule` function in the following code snippet is provided to create a binding between the pod and a node. The `Bind` method is called under the pod in `clientset` in the last line of the function since it is a subresource of a pod:

```
func schedule(pod, node, namespace string) error {
    fmt.Printf("Assigning %s/%s to %s\n", namespace, pod, node)
    // Create a binding with pod and node
    binding := v1.Binding{
        ObjectMeta: metav1.ObjectMeta{
            Name: pod,
        },
        Target: v1.ObjectReference{
            Kind: "Node",
            APIVersion: "v1",
            Name: node,
        }}
    return clientset.CoreV1().Pods(namespace).Bind(&binding)
}
```

This custom scheduler randomly assigns nodes to the pods with the custom scheduler named `packt-scheduler`. The build files and documentation are provided under the `k8s-scheduler-example` folder, and are ready to be deployed to the cluster. In the following section, the deployment and use of multiple schedulers in a Kubernetes cluster will be presented.

Deploying and using a Custom Kubernetes Scheduler

Consider, a client has a Kubernetes cluster and requires an additional scheduler for the pods with predefined labels. The new scheduler should work side-by-side with the built-in scheduler, and it should be deployed to the cluster. We'll deploy and use a custom Kubernetes scheduler and check how the schedulers work in the cluster. We need to ensure that the following steps are completed before deploying a Kubernetes scheduler:

- Use the random assignment scheduler from this exercise.
- The scheduler container is already in Docker hub: `onuryilmaz/k8sscheduler-example`.
- Use `packt-scheduler` as the custom scheduler name.
- Show the status of the pods if the custom scheduler is not running.

 You can find the `pod.yaml` file at: `https://goo.gl/aCRppt`.

Let's begin with the implementation:

1. Create a pod with the custom scheduler name, defined as `packt-scheduler`:

   ```
   kubectl apply -f k8s-scheduler-example/deploy/pod.yaml
   ```

   After deploying the pod, its status can be checked:

   ```
   kubectl get pods
   ```

   You should see the following output:

   Since there is no scheduler deployed to the cluster with the name `packt-scheduler`, its status will be stuck as `Pending` forever.

2. Deploy the scheduler into the cluster with the following command:

```
kubectl apply -f k8s-scheduler-example/deploy/scheduler.yaml
```

 You can find the `scheduler.yaml` file at: `https://goo.gl/AaSu8o`.

3. Check the pods with the following command:

```
kubectl get pods
```

You'll get the following output:

As shown previously, the scheduler runs in a pod and, in addition, the `nginx` pod, which was Pending before, now has the `Running` status.

4. In addition, check the logs of the scheduler:

```
kubectl logs scheduler
```

You'll get the following output:

```
$ kubectl logs scheduler
Starting scheduler: packt-scheduler
Assigning default/nginx to minikube
$
```

5. Run the following command for cleaning up:

```
kubectl delete -f k8s-scheduler-example/deploy/pod.yaml
kubectl delete -f k8s-scheduler-example/deploy/scheduler.yaml
```

Extending Kubernetes Infrastructure

Kubernetes clusters are run on actual bare-metal clusters and interact with the infrastructure systems running on the servers. Extension points for infrastructure are still in the design stage and not mature enough for standardization. However, they can be grouped as follows:

- **Server**: The Kubernetes node components interact with container runtimes such as Docker. Currently, Kubernetes is designed to work with any container runtime that implements the **Container Runtime Interface (CRI)** specification. CRI consists of libraries, protocol buffers, and the gRPC API to define the interaction between Kubernetes and the container environment.
- **Network**: Kubernetes and the container architecture requires high-performance networking, decoupled from container runtime. The connections between containers and network interfaces are defined with the abstraction of the **Container Network Interface (CNI)**. The CNI consists of a set of interfaces for adding and removing containers from the Kubernetes network.
- **Storage**: Storage for Kubernetes resources is provided by the storage plugins that are communicating with cloud providers or the host system. For instance, a Kubernetes cluster running on AWS could easily get storage from AWS and attach to its stateful sets. Operations including storage provisioning and consuming in container runtimes are standardized under the **Container Storage Interface (CSI)**. In Kubernetes, any storage plugin implementing CSI can be used as a storage provider.

The infrastructure of Kubernetes can be extended to work with servers implementing CRI, network providers compliant with CNI, and storage providers realizing CSI.

Summary

In this chapter, extending Kubernetes was covered, where we enabled converting domain expertise into automation and intervening Kubernetes operations. Firstly, the extension points in Kubernetes were presented to show its built-in extension capabilities. Throughout the chapter, new resources were added to the Kubernetes API, and their operations were automated so that Kubernetes can work for custom resources in addition to the built-in ones. Following this, resource creation logic was extended with dynamic admission controllers, and you were shown how to include operational requirements in the Kubernetes API resource life cycle.

Finally, configuring the scheduler of Kubernetes was presented to cover all extensive requirements for nodes and inter-pod relations. How to write, deploy, and use a custom scheduler was also shown. With the extension capabilities included in this chapter, it is possible to use Kubernetes, not only as a container orchestrator, but as a platform capable of handling all custom requirements of cloud-native applications.

In this book, Kubernetes design patterns and extensions were presented from their foundations to their implementations in a cloud-native microservice architecture. Firstly, in the first chapter, best practices for Kubernetes were covered. Design patterns and their reflections on the cloud-native architecture of Kubernetes were illustrated in order to create best practice knowledge. In the second chapter, how to connect to Kubernetes programmatically was presented. The hands-on activities on client libraries were aimed at being ready for the applications that communicate with Kubernetes. These Kubernetes API consuming applications will make a difference for utilizing Kubernetes and enable achieving more than a casual Kubernetes user. In the last chapter, Kubernetes extension points were covered. Kubernetes extension points enable converting domain expertise into automation and intervening Kubernetes operations. With the extension capabilities included in this last chapter, it is possible to use Kubernetes, not only as a container orchestrator, but as a platform capable of handling the complex requirements of cloud-native applications.

Solutions

This section contains the worked-out answers for the activities present in each lesson. Note that in case of descriptive questions, your answers might not match the ones provided in this section completely. As long as the essence of the answers remain the same, you can consider them correct.

Chapter 1: Kubernetes Design Patterns

Following are the activity solutions for this chapter.

Activity: Running a Web Server with Synchronization

In the `sidecar.yaml` file, pod definition with two containers, namely `server` and `sync`, is provided. In the server container, httpd serves the source volume on port 80. In the sync container, git runs with every 30 seconds to synchronize the source volume. These two containers work independently; however, they are sharing the source volume to achieve file synchronization:

```
apiVersion: v1
kind: Pod
metadata:
      name: sidecar
spec:
    containers:
...
volumes:
- emptyDir: {}
   name: source
```

Follow these steps to get the solution:

1. Create the pod with the following command:

```
kubectl apply -f sidecar.yaml
```

2. Check whether the pod is ready with the name sidecar:

```
kubectl get pod sidecar
```

3. When the pod is ready, check the logs of synchronization sidecar container:

```
kubectl logs sidecar -c sync
```

4. Forward the server port of the pod to localhost with the following command:

```
kubectl port-forward sidecar 8000:80
```

5. Open localhost:8000 in the browser. It is expected to see a 2048 game.

Activity: Running a Web Server after Content Preparation

In the init-container.yaml file, pod definition with one initialization and one main container, namely content and server, is provided. In the content container, "Welcome from Packt" is written into the index file. In the server container, nginx serves the source volume on port 80. These two containers work independently; however, they are sharing the workdir volume to achieve file preparation:

```
apiVersion: v1
kind: Pod
metadata:
      name: init-container
spec:
    initContainers:
    -
    ...
volumes:
- name: workdir
    emptyDir: {}
```

Follow these steps to get the solution:

1. Create the pod with the following command:

   ```
   kubectl apply -f init-container.yaml
   ```

2. Check the state of the initialization container:

   ```
   kubectl describe pod init-container
   ```

3. When the pod is running, forward the server port of the pod to localhost with the following command:

   ```
   kubectl port-forward init-container 8000:80
   ```

4. In another terminal, check the content of the server with the following command:

   ```
   curl localhost:8000
   ```

5. Run the following command for cleanup:

   ```
   kubectl delete deployment go-client
   ```

Activity: Injecting Data into Applications

In the `inject.yaml` file, there is a pod definition with one container that logs its runtime information in every 10 seconds. Resource requests and limits are defined for memory and cpu for utilization and performance information.
Environment variables are defined with `valueFrom` blocks which shows that values are filled during runtime:

Follow these steps to get the solution:

1. Create the pod with the following command:

   ```
   kubectl apply -f inject.yaml
   ```

2. Check whether the inject pod is ready:

   ```
   kubectl get pod inject
   ```

3. When the pod is ready, check the logs:

   ```
   kubectl logs inject
   ```

Chapter 2: Kubernetes Client Libraries

Following are the activity solutions for this chapter.

Activity: Using the Kubernetes Go Client inside the Cluster

1. Create a deployment with the Docker image of the example client from the previous exercise:

   ```
   kubectl run go-client --image=onuryilmaz/k8s-clientexample:go
   ```

2. Wait until the pod is running by using the following command:

   ```
   kubectl get pods -w
   ```

3. Get the logs of the deployment pod with the following command:

   ```
   kubectl logs $(kubectl get pods --selector run=go-client -o
   jsonpath="{.items[0].metadata.name}")
   ```

Other Books You May Enjoy

If you enjoyed this book, you may be interested in these other books by Packt:

Getting Started with Kubernetes - Second Edition
Jonathan Baier

ISBN: 978-1-78728-336-7

- Download, install, and configure the Kubernetes codebase
  Understand the core concepts of a Kubernetes cluster
- Be able to set up and access monitoring and logging for Kubernetes cluster
- Set up external access to applications running in the cluster
- Understand how CoreOS and Kubernetes can help you achieve greater
  performance and container implementation agility
- Run multiple clusters and manage from a single control plane
- Explore container security as well as securing Kubernetes clusters
- Work with third-party extensions and tools

Mastering Kubernetes
Gigi Sayfan

ISBN: 978-1-78646-100-1

- Architect a robust Kubernetes cluster for long-time operation
- Discover the advantages of running Kubernetes on GCE, AWS, Azure, and bare metal
- See the identity model of Kubernetes and options for cluster federation
- Monitor and troubleshoot Kubernetes clusters and run a highly available Kubernetes
- Create and configure custom Kubernetes resources and use third-party resources in your automation workflows
- Discover the art of running complex stateful applications in your container environment
- Deliver applications as standard packages

Leave a Review - Let Other Readers Know What You Think

Please share your thoughts on this book with others by leaving a review on the site that you bought it from. If you purchased the book from Amazon, please leave us an honest review on this book's Amazon page. This is vital so that other potential readers can see and use your unbiased opinion to make purchasing decisions, we can understand what our customers think about our products, and our authors can see your feedback on the title that they have worked with Packt to create. It will only take a few minutes of your time, but is valuable to other potential customers, our authors, and Packt. Thank you!

Index

V

vendoring 46

W

web server
  running, after content preparation 14, 15
  running, with synchronization 12

www.ingramcontent.com/pod-product-compliance
Lightning Source LLC
Chambersburg PA
CBHW080540060326
40690CB00022B/5185